FORTUNATE

Trigger Warnings: Suicide, postnatal depression, grief, objectification, sexual harassment, anxiety, miscarriage, weight.

Not suitable for younger readers.

Copyright © 2024 J. D. Fields

All rights reserved. No part of this book may be reproduced or used in any manner without the prior written permission of the copyright owner, except for the use of brief quotations in a book review.

Paperback: 9798343654288

First paperback edition: November 2024

Cover art by Zoe Lewis and J. D. Fields
Editing and formatting by Faith Fawcett

This book is dedicated to my family and friends, who have supported me through every adventure and hurdle. I especially want to thank my mum and husband; you are my biggest cheerleaders. Finally, to my son, Frankie. You have taught me so much about myself and I hope, when you read this one day, you'll be proud of your mum.

Contents

7 Author's Note

9 Chapter 1 – Sexual Breasty Object
25 Chapter 2 – Mission Tits
39 Chapter 3 – Getting my Shit Together
45 Chapter 4 – Prince Charming
57 Chapter 5 – A Year to Remember
67 Chapter 6 – When the World Turned Upside Down
83 Chapter 7 – After Every Storm comes the Rainbow
99 Chapter 8 – The Day that Time Stood Still
111 Chapter 9 – A New Chapter
125 Chapter 10 – Postnatal Depression Label Not Required
135 Chapter 11 – Whirlwind Emotions
153 Chapter 12 – Lost in Torment
175 Chapter 13 – Found in Freedom
185 Chapter 14 – A New Path
201 Chapter 15 – A Letter to Uncle Kev

207 Support Contacts

209 Citations

Author's Introduction

My life is nothing extravagant, exciting or shocking… so if I were you, I'd stop reading now.

I joke!

But seriously, everyone has a story worth telling.

I started writing this as a twenty-nine-year-old mother of a handsome little boy, a very soon-to-be wife of the man of her dreams, and a hardworking student studying for the job she had always aspired to do. By the time I finish writing this, I will hopefully be a wife — if he shows up!

Okay, enough sarcasm now.

I am so fortunate for all that I have in my life. This book is a rollercoaster journey of emotions, and there are areas addressed that I feel less fortunate for happening but stronger for.

If any of the topics discussed relate to your own experiences, I hope you can find comfort in knowing you are not alone. There is always help.

I hope you enjoy reading my story so far.

Chapter 1
Sexual Breasty Object

My breasts, *oh my Lord!*
A considerable weight to bear.

We are a family of big-chested women, although mine are ridiculously big. From the age of nine, when I began to develop, I hated them! At secondary school, I was known as 'big tits Jazz', sexualised from day one of year seven at only eleven years old. Boys in my year would make remarks and ask for pictures (they never got any). And countless times, I was even groped as they walked by.

The thing is, I never thought this was wrong as it had begun at such a young age and became somewhat the norm for me. To be honest, once a grope of my breasts had taken place, the incident would leave my mind as quickly as the act had occurred; I painfully normalised it.

Being a tomboy who was and still is madly into football, my breasts were a problem when it came to playing the game with boys my age. I found myself fitting in less with the lads who I enjoyed a kick about with because their attitude towards me changed when puberty hit. I had female friends at school, but very few girls shared my interest in football, and the ones that did would only play when we were training for the school team or playing matches. So, I began to do the
same: I would hang around with girls more and became less of a tomboy.

...

When I was in year nine, I started my first job at the age of thirteen: pot washing at the pub in the village next to ours. My sister, who is two years older than me, was a waitress there, so she helped me get the job.

My sister and I couldn't be more different. Her interests have always been academic, and she loves the outdoors. Meanwhile, mine were more focused on socialising, partying, and being the class clown. Nowadays, her idea of a good time is to be like Bear Grylls, hiking somewhere and camping. Mine is to be out bottomless brunching and dancing to old cheesy pop—*chalk and cheese.*

At thirteen, I became interested in fashion, hair and makeup, like most girls that age. However, I was still very much into football and played every week for my local girl's team and school team. But makeup became part of my everyday routine, even for school. I used to steal my mum's foundation and she would go ballistic when it was nearly all gone after a week! Although, that never stopped me from using as much as I did, much to my mum's annoyance.

With a face full, I always looked older than my age, especially with giant boobs; I could easily pass for sixteen, which, at that age, I thought was great.

So, my pot-washing job began to pay for my makeup obsession.

I enjoyed my little job. A few of the chefs who worked there were lads who were around five years older than me, but they were able to chat with me easily because they had younger siblings and were used to it.

The landlord seemed alright, but I never saw much of him as I only worked pot washing once or twice a week in the kitchen corner. When he would come in, he was pleasant, but I found his eye contact to be slightly intense at times.

One weekend, I was asked to work a Saturday daytime shift as one of the chefs was ill, and they needed an extra pair of hands peeling vegetables and washing pots. I didn't mind doing extra jobs around the kitchen; a change from cleaning dishes was always welcome, even though I never really minded that either. I often asked if there was anything else I could do to help during shifts that weren't busy.

I have never been one to stand around and do the minimum when it comes to work, but I can't say I have always had that attitude towards academics.

Returning to the Saturday I mentioned, I came in to help. The boss entered the kitchen, chatting with the chefs following the mad lunchtime rush. He said that my wages were in his office if I wanted to go and get them, which I did, of course. I always looked forward to getting my wages and planning how I would spend them every week. Usually, this was on the infamous Dream Matte Mousse foundation, which was the craze when I was younger.

Once in his office, he sat in his chair and went to his desk drawer for my wages. I had noticed pictures of various aircraft on the wall, something I have always been mesmerised by. He'd observed my interest and began talking to me about them. It had been a conversation I'd enjoyed, and I hadn't felt uneasy.

But then, when there was nothing left to discuss regarding planes, he sat back into his chair and began making the creepy eye contact I was not a fan of, along with an awkward silence. I didn't know what to say other than:

"My mum will be here soon; I should get ready to go".

He had held out the envelope with my wages in his hand for me to take. As I had gone to grab them, he'd moved his hand back towards himself and asked for a kiss.

Gross!

I had no idea what to say or do. He was around fifty years of age with a big thick porn star moustache, and he dressed worse than my grandad. Put it this way: he was no Ashton Merrygold from JLS (he was probably my crush for the week then).

So I'd stood there, looking at him blank-faced, until I opened my mouth and the words "I need a wee" spilt out. I left quickly, went to the toilet, and did not step back into his office *again.*

I had been confused and didn't know where to put myself; thank God my shift was nearly over! I'd left the toilet cautiously and returned to the kitchen, where my wage packet was sitting on the side near the washing-up area. But he had been nowhere to be seen. I grabbed the envelope, said bye to the chefs quickly and left.

I remember asking my sister later that day if she thought the boss was weird. She'd said," Not really," and I did not elaborate. I felt uneasy working there after that encounter, but thankfully, he'd never asked me to go into his office again.

I'd avoided his creepy eye contact by simply not looking in his direction when he spoke with the chefs and by keeping my head down when he said hello. I'd hated the way it had made me feel and how it had ruined my little job.

Not long after, my aunt's friend offered me a job as a Saturday girl at a hair salon in town, and I left the pub. I had just turned fourteen and was moving up in the world from washing pots to washing hair. The salon was where my passion for makeup and dressing nicely fitted in, rather than in a kitchen. I immensely enjoyed the job and meeting different people all the time; it was so interesting, and every shift was always different.

...

My hobby had always been football, but I had bionic breasts that wouldn't allow physical activity much past the age of fourteen. They took my passion away from me!

I had visited the doctor because I thought my heart was playing up. I would all of a sudden get a sharp pain that would take my breath away. Thankfully, there weren't any implications with my heart causing me pain.

However, it had turned out to be the size of my breasts pulling on the muscles around my heart, and I would grab my left boob, lifting it in an attempt to take the straining pain away when it occurred.

I was a 34GG at this point, and they just kept growing!

And, by fifteen, it's fair to say it felt normal for boys to place their hands on me without consent.

It's sad to look back now and know I felt this way even back then. If a young girl said to me now that they thought it was normal for the opposite sex to touch her breasts without consent, I would be horrified and tell her it is absolutely not normal and is unacceptable.

Still, fourteen years ago, consent wasn't as big of a topic as it has been recently, so I was none the wiser.

I remember the first time I was aware it wasn't right for boys to touch my chest as they pleased. It was sports day; I was in year ten and had just turned fifteen. A female teacher saw a boy from the year above me come up behind me, reach around and grope my breasts. The teacher was horrified.

I was not.

She went ballistic at him and sent him to the head teacher's office, giving him multiple detentions.

I also received a letter of apology from him, which she had obviously made part of his punishment. This was the first out of countless times a person from the opposite sex had put his hands on me, and the first time it made me feel like it was wrong.

...

We went on a family holiday to Turkey in the summer when I was fifteen.

While on holiday, a member of the entertainment staff had become quite friendly with our family and did not imply sexualised behaviour towards me. A man in a position of trust with kids! I liked him; he was funny and made everyone he spoke to laugh.

One day, he had told me to come to the beach after lunch as he had organised a few water activities for teenagers staying at the hotel.

My sister and stepbrother didn't seem to have been told or invited, but they were two years older than me, so I didn't think much of it. I probably thought they were too cool to be doing teenage activities when they were about to turn into adults themselves. I got the 'OK' from my mum and went off to the beach.

When I got there, I couldn't see anyone I recognised. It had been bustling, but the hotel was huge and could accommodate many guests. I walked further down and saw the hotel's entertainment guy in the water; he waved, telling me to come in. I hadn't thought twice; I just went.

Once in the water, the waves had been quite choppy, and I wasn't the strongest of swimmers, but I got by.

Treading water, I'd drifted out and looked around for others, but only he was there. He was well-built and the water felt no match for him.

He had swum over to me fast, grabbed the backs of my thighs, placing them around him. He had told me how beautiful I was and how my body turned him on so much. He had also said he didn't have long so we needed to be quick.

I was in shock. I could feel him against me; his genitals had been lined up to mine and pressing into me through my bikini bottoms. He'd attempted to move them, but I had found my voice at this point. I'd asked him to stop, but his grip became tighter. I was looking around, but no one was close by.

How the fuck had I got there?

I'd begun to struggle, and then a big wave came.

Thank God.

We had gone under, and it separated us.

I swam as fast as I could without looking back, going toward the shore and towards *people*. I'd got out of the sea, went straight up to my hotel room and threw up. I'd looked in the mirror and cried.

What the hell had just happened to me?

I still acted so young at fifteen, maybe too young, but I let my older sister do everything for me; I didn't need to grow up.

Don't get me wrong, I was no angel, and I thought that I was all grown up with my mates when we stole wine from one of their mum's stashes and got very drunk in the park. My mum had found out and I was very much grounded for what felt like forever. But that didn't stop me from doing stuff like drinking with my friends again and generally pushing boundaries like most teens do.

Back in the hotel room, I'd changed my clothes and then returned to the pool area where my mum was, but I never spoke about what had happened.

At dinner that evening, he came over and laughed with my family like he had done most evenings when we had been there. I couldn't laugh like I had before. He was suddenly not funny anymore.

I got up and excused myself for the toilet. When I left the bathroom, he was waiting outside and told me not to say anything or else he would lose his job. I agreed and said I wouldn't say anything.

I kept that promise.

Until now.

I have always been close to my mum and can tell her everything. I would have no problem talking to her about boys. But when it came to these incidents with older men that I didn't really understand myself, it felt somewhat of a challenge to voice. So, I just didn't.

I've never liked drama, so I've always tried to steer clear of it. But, suppose I could go back and tell myself to report what he had attempted to do. Who knows? I may have saved some other young girl from experiencing the same encounter I had been lucky enough to swim away from.

...

When I started back at school following the Turkey holiday, I was in my final year and had pushed that incident with the entertainment man out of my mind.

I had left my Saturday job at the salon to 'concentrate better before exams'. However, I really just enjoyed meeting my mates on a weekend and going into town.

Halfway through year eleven, I had boobs that were overpowering but also desperation to find a place in the world. Midwifery had been a brief thought, but only because I didn't believe I could do it academically.

Maybe the size of my boobs had taken away from the size of my brain?

Also, sex education freaked me out at school when it came to diagrams of women's reproductive organs and words like 'cervix' and 'ovaries' made me wince for years. I would sit in class while the teacher would be describing a woman's menstrual cycle and go white as a ghost. Then, I would be excused from the class due to looking like Casper (the friendly ghost). It was all very dramatic.

In my GCSE exams, I did alright but nowhere near well enough for A-Levels, so I said goodbye to my Midwifery idea. I had already partly let go of it anyway due to my little tolerance for female reproductive organs.

I went on to do hairdressing at college instead. I had enjoyed it and made some fantastic friends. I was also pretty good at styling and colouring women's hair.

The girls in my class would practise on each other, and I would leave a day of learning with hairstyles that looked like I was ready to go to a ball. We also practised haircuts and colouring on each other; I loved it.

Over the two years I studied hairdressing, my hair had all sorts of different shades of highlights. Most weeks, I would have a new colour or style.

...

I had begun working at a pub in the evenings and weekends around college (a different one from when I was thirteen). I loved it! Well, *most* of the time. I felt like I had found my place in the world, a big statement for a seventeen-year-old!

When I began working there, I was no longer addressed as a child; I was now a woman. I felt so grown up. I'd found confidence in talking to different personalities and my ability to make people laugh; it was something that I had always done, but my humour altered with adult conversations.

Men noticed me: young, middle-aged, old... it didn't matter.

This was the first time that I had felt beautiful and fancied; I thought that it meant that I was in control. I look back now and call it young, naive, and impressionable.

While working there, I passed my driving test and completed my practical test the first time. Yet, my theory took a few goes, highlighting my practical learning strengths compared to written tasks.

On the second attempt at the theory exam, I turned up late, hungover, unshowered, and wearing sunglasses. I'd passed by one point! I'm not sure how I managed it, but I wasn't going to question it.

After passing my test and getting a car, my job description had somehow evolved into becoming a regular taxi drop-off for drunks, usually at the request of my boss, who enjoyed the punters staying as he was making money.

Sometimes, I had felt very uneasy with the characters I would have in my car; unwanted sexual remarks and even a few passes were made at me, but the word '*NO!*' seemed to be understood, luckily.

I worked there with incidents like those mentioned until age twenty.

I sometimes question if I was too friendly or naive, blaming myself when I know that I shouldn't. I can't say I hadn't enjoyed *some* of the attention, though; it was nice to feel like I was desired.

...

Back then, we are talking eleven years ago; there seemed to be this narrative that if a woman has large breasts, they are there for others' entertainment. Well, that's how I felt anyway.

But the world has evolved since then, and women's voices are being heard. Some women are only just understanding and realising that they have previously been victims of inappropriate sexual behaviours that didn't seem much at the time. Also, over the last decade or so, I have learnt that we, as females, are not actually objects for male enjoyment.

I'm sure every woman has their story to tell about sexual abuse, discrimination, harassment and misconduct. If they don't - they are lucky.

The sad thing is that it has taken women to be hurt, raped and killed for awareness of how male behaviours impact female lives.

Take Sarah Everard, for example, a beautiful young woman from London who lost her life after being kidnapped, raped and killed at the hands of a male police officer and a complete stranger to her.

Shocking, isn't it?

Many reported in the media on how violence against women greatly impacted females' day-to-day lives and how it, in turn, made us more vigilant when walking the streets or when we were out socialising.

These despicable acts have highlighted to the nation the consciousness of males' inappropriate actions, the ones that affect females.

Women are becoming more aware of what is right and wrong when it comes to their bodies; women are standing up against belittling and assaulting behaviours; women are becoming more powerful through knowledge, empowerment and standing by one another.

...

At twenty, I began a new role in a school kitchen and formed a relationship with the chef at the pub that I had resigned from only weeks earlier.

He was a nice guy, but he was eight years older than me. He had two kids and a messy relationship background, but I was desperate to be in a relationship, feeling wanted not just in a sexual way but in *every* way.

But it was too much, too young.

I had moved in with him very quickly, even though we weren't right for each other. We had also become an item under complex circumstances and clashed as we were at very different points in our lives.

I became overweight, and my breasts were still climbing the tape measure.

That summer, my friends and I had already planned for a girls' holiday before I got into a relationship.

I couldn't have been less excited about going if I had tried. I felt like one massive frump and had no idea where I was going to find swimwear or nice evening outfits to fit my oddly shaped body. It wasn't in proportion, and back then, I compared my shape to an upside-down pear.

My fat distribution does not go lower than my love handles, and back then, my upper body was around three dress sizes bigger. I hid my huge 38KK breasts underneath baggy clothes; that was my comfort.

Despite all those factors that made me hate myself, that holiday was fantastic! It was my first girl's holiday, and I loved it. I'd forgotten about my physical and mental struggles, and I simply enjoyed life. I'd been present, and in the moment, I even found nice and comfortable outfits to wear in the extreme heat.

But, coming back to reality had hit like a tonne of bricks. I had MAJOR holiday blues. Deep down, I knew that I was unhappy in my relationship, but I needed to tackle one thing at a time.

My breasts were my priority.

I had gone to the GP again, who referred me to a breast consultant; they had examined my chest and informed me that he agreed that I needed breast reduction surgery. They were causing all kinds of issues with me, physically and mentally.

He had even stated that I would become a cripple as I was starting to accumulate curvature of the spine.

Just what every young girl wants to hear.

Still, the criteria for the surgery had been so tight that he knew it would be rejected. But we proceeded with the application anyway. And, as he predicted, it was a big fat rejection.

I had been to the GP before about a breast reduction when I was sixteen, but the NHS declined me then, too. They told me that I did not meet the criteria and that my breasts would not stop growing till I was twenty-one anyway.

After my appointment with the consultant, I became depressed. But mental health, back then, wasn't as big of a topic as it is today; I just plodded through life and began to accept that this was me.

I ate for comfort and had started to avoid mirrors. I wore size twenty tops to accommodate my large breasts and expanding waistline.

I couldn't face the fact that I was unhappy in the relationship because I was just unhappy altogether.

Who would want me now?

I was a woman who was destined to be a cripple.

I had continued to carry on in the same relationship, and the same job with the same poor mental health that had never been addressed, and I was declining by the week.

But, there was a turning point.

I had planned to meet two of my friends for dinner one evening, and this is where hope began to creep in.

Chapter 2
Mission Tits

I had met my friends for dinner at a restaurant in the town centre. It was about a ten-minute walk from where I lived with my partner, so having a few drinks was no issue.

The two friends I'd met that night were aware of my struggles with my breasts and continuous battle with the NHS to help me. I look back now and think that if I had divulged how I was feeling to the NHS about my poor mental health, maybe they would have done something. But, like I said in the previous chapter, the topic of mental health was not as accepted as it is now, and there was a lack of awareness around it compared to today.

During dinner, one of my friends had said that she had something to tell me. Of course, I was utterly drawn. I eagerly replied, "What, what, what?" to which she told me that her mum had got back from Lithuania a month prior and had breast reduction surgery whilst out there.

OH MY GOODNESS.

I was speechless; going abroad had never been on my radar, as you hear so many horror stories of botched plastic surgery. I also remember the consultant from my last appointment regarding my breasts, who had warned me never to go abroad for surgery.

But, once the information my friend had just disclosed had sunk in, I asked a tone of questions about her mum's experience and recovery.

I began planning my own trip in my head whilst drinking celebratory gin and tonics because I instantly knew that this was the answer to my problems.

This information put a spring in my step for the next few days, even though I had made no headway in doing anything. I needed to gather more research to present the idea of going to my mum.

When I decided it was time to talk to her, I drove to her house and recited my pitch in the car like I was about to walk into Alan Sugars' boardroom; I certainly did not want to be fired! Not that my mum was unapproachable in the slightest, but I knew that she would be hard to convince that going abroad for surgery would be a good idea, especially after what the consultant had said.

Standing in her kitchen, I relayed all the information my friend had told me about her mum and the research I had gathered. *Pleadingly.*

I told her not to give me an answer immediately and to think about it and let it sink in. I saw on her face that she didn't like the idea at first, but I was desperate; I did not want to spiral further into physical and mental hell.

I remember saying to her a few days after, "I'm doing this with or without you, but I would much prefer to do it with you." It gave her no choice in trying to talk me out of it.

She was very sceptical, as most mums would be. Still, it wasn't as though I needed her permission to leave the country and undergo this operation; I was an adult.

But despite that fact, I needed her. I needed her support, and I needed her there with me. There wasn't anyone else whom I wanted more.

Soon after, I contacted the same Lithuanian plastic surgery clinic my friend's mum had used. To say I was booking to undergo one of the most life-changing events for me, the process was pretty straightforward.

It felt too good to be true.

I liaised with a woman from the clinic over email for several months, working out the logistics of my trip, surgery and aftercare. My dad was fantastic and gave me considerable financial help towards it.

In contrast, my original plan was to get a loan and consider the consequences later; a well-thought-out plan, if you ask me.

My mum, the logistical superstar, took care of everything other than the surgery. She booked and paid for the flights and accommodation and made sure that it was suitable for a woman who had just undergone breast surgery. So much credit is owed to my parents, especially regarding this whirlwind experience.

My parents had split when I was five; my mum had met someone else who became my stepdad and still is. But they didn't let that faze their co-parenting, and what a fucking team they were for my sister and me (and still are).

We were obviously devastated and heartbroken that our parents were separating. Still, they made the transition with as much ease as possible for us.

The parent team excelled themselves without them knowing when it came to the surgery; this was mainly due to me feeling comfortable that they had everything covered, leaving me with no worries and fully able to concentrate on the operation to come.

In March 2016, just before the referendum and my twenty-first birthday, my mum and I took off for Lithuania.

I would hate to think how much the surgery would have been after Britain left the European Union. I feel lucky that we managed to get there before Brexit won.

When we landed at Vilnius airport, a female driver from the clinic picked us up and drove us to Kaunas, where our accommodation and the clinic were situated.

The driver was a nice young lady who spoke English fluently. She answered the *many* questions we had on the hour-long transfer to Kaunas.

The surgery was scheduled for the day after we arrived, and thankfully, the clinic was not far from where we were staying. All thanks to my mum and her planning. *Superstar.*

We headed straight to the clinic from the airport, where I had blood tests and a general health check.

I was given my pre-op instructions for the next day, which included not eating after 05:30 in the morning. My surgery was planned for 17:30 that evening, and it was the longest day of my life. Not only was I beginning to feel slightly nervous and excited, but I was also bloody hungry, and I definitely do not do well on an empty stomach: hangry witch comes to mind.

When I arrived at the clinic on the big day, I'd chatted with the surgeon before the surgery, and it felt surreal. I stood in front of the surgeon while he drew all over my chest, chatting away.

There were so many pen marks, and I felt like he was constructing an architectural drawing. I suppose, in a way, he was. It was the oddest, most awkward, but exciting experience I have ever endured.

I remember sitting in my gown in the room that was allocated to me, ready to go into surgery. I looked down at my breasts and thought to myself, *bye fuckers*. I thought about all the clothes I could buy and all the things I would be able to do without them weighing me down... like running!

It had been years since I felt that I had moved faster than even a sloth at this point.

A blonde, long-haired nurse entered my room and put a cannula in my hand. She was a lovely lady. I remember her settling my nerves by being quite jovial when inserting it and administering some medication.

She gave me a drug, which made me feel drunk, and then my mum began to get emotional. It was as though a sudden realisation had just hit her: this was really happening.

Once the effects of that drug started to kick in, I was told that I needed to say goodbye to my mum and follow the nurse into the theatre room.

Saying bye to her was horrible; she was an emotional wreck, and I felt spaced out. I suppose that the medication the nurse had given me before going into the theatre was to relax me, as I can imagine walking in there could make anyone about to undergo an operation have a panic attack.

I got up onto the surgical table and lay down. The last thing I remember is the surgical team putting a quilt over my legs, which I could feel was annoying my toes.

My last *thought* was to move it, but suddenly, it was no longer a problem, and everything went dark.

Following the surgery, I woke up in recovery, feeling like I had been hit by a bus after the most extensive drinking session of my life.

I had a drain coming out from underneath my bandages on each breast, which grossed me out, and I kept vomiting due to the medication in my system. Overall, I had felt very weak and shaky.

I pressed the buzzer next to my hand, and the same nurse who had cannulated me came in and helped me get to the toilet. I felt horrendous. It took everything I had to get out of bed, go to the bathroom and back.

I don't remember much about the room I had stayed in but that could be a good thing.

I managed to sleep all night and was woken in the morning with a round of toast that took about half an hour to eat and a hot drink.

The surgeon came in to see how I was doing and said he was happy with the operation. However, I was slightly shocked to find out that I was to be discharged before lunch, less than twenty-four hours after breast reduction surgery.

I had no idea how I was supposed to leave the clinic feeling like a zombie from *The Walking Dead*.

Soon after, the nurse came in to take the drains out. I was given a bag of tablets and several appointments over the next five days to attend for checkups. And then, I was sent on my way.

Back at the accommodation, my mum suddenly took on the role of nurse.

She gave me my medication at the exact time it was due and ensured I had everything I needed to be as comfy and well-rested as possible.

When it came to toileting and personal hygiene, she didn't bat an eye and assisted me with everything! She even had to wipe my bum because the stretch of reaching around pulled on my chest. *Lucky woman!* There was nothing she wouldn't do.

While in our accommodation, I lay in bed most days watching Netflix on my partner's iPad, which he had lent me. As I mentioned, he was genuinely lovely, but we were very different people. He had trust issues due to a previous relationship breakdown that he inflicted on ours. We often argued, but that's because we wanted different things out of life.

I believe we were both stubborn in hanging on to each other as it seemed that he couldn't be alone, and I didn't want to be, no matter how miserable we were together.

He knew how men would talk to me when working at the pub because that's where he worked, too. He sometimes made remarks that I was a tart and liked the attention, but that was his insecurities talking.

After the operation, I remember messaging him from Lithuania, talking about how I couldn't wait to wear and do new things. His reply was the oddest thing. His message was, "Really! You're already planning how you can show them off to men?"

What the fuck!

Was he fucking serious?

I knew that I wanted to leave him, and I admitted it to myself. I should have left when returning from Lithuania, but I didn't because I couldn't face that mess while feeling so vulnerable. Looking back, it would have done us both a favour.

In Lithuania, I attended my appointments at the clinic over the next five days to check my wounds. The surgeon was pleased with how they were healing, even though when my bandages came off so that he could observe, the colour of my chest was all shades of dark purples and yellows from the bruising, and the pain level matched the intensity of the bruising.

Ouch.

It was disturbing to see, but it was part of the process.

When it was time to travel back home, my mum had taken on the role of luggage lady, carrying everything so I didn't have to. There's nothing that this woman won't do.

The plane journey was horrendous. It was uncomfortable and was physically and mentally draining. I couldn't focus on anything else other than the throbbing pain in my chest, which seemed to be more intense at the higher altitude.

When I arrived home and returned to my partner's house, I began my actual recovery process, which included very light household duties and lounging around for much of the day for the next six weeks.

I was on top of changing my dressings and cleaning my wounds, and my partner was good at helping me redress them. The clinic offered no guidance on how often I should change them, so I did them daily.

However, little did I know that it was the wrong thing to be doing.

I eventually accumulated an infection in my left breast because of how frequently the wounds were being exposed. I began with flu-like symptoms: I was shivering and unable to get warm.

As I lay in bed, waking from a nap, I found my left side drenched in clear liquid. I panicked. I immediately phoned my mum, who told me to call the GP, and I got an appointment immediately, surprisingly.

My nan on my dad's side was great. She was on hand to pick me up and drive me to the GP practice. She has always been there when I've needed something at the drop of a hat. She is such a sweet soul and a true angel.

On my visit to the GP, I had discovered that the incision point underneath my left breast had a deep hole where the infection was. It was a gruesome sight where you could see internal breast tissue.

Disgusting.

This was when the NHS began to take over my wound care.

The GP that I saw around two weeks post-operation, who gave me the diagnosis of infection, was a stern-looking woman. It was an awful and judgemental experience. I remember her words: "You silly, silly girl, why did you go abroad for this operation? We now have to pick up the pieces of what we have no record of."

Wow! What a bitch she was.

I could understand her view of the situation's inconvenience, but that was minuscule compared to my frustrations with it. Besides, I didn't need to forgive her for the way that she had handled the situation; it was unprofessional, to say the least.

But I had no energy to care what she thought, so I gave her silence in return. It was partly because I had no energy to defend myself, but it was also because I thought that she was a twat.

I will never forget that encounter with her.

She had no idea the hell that I had been through and where desperation had got me.

Fuck her opinion.

I didn't need to justify myself to anyone, let alone someone who had just met me.

However, she did book me in every week for the next six weeks to see the nurse practitioner who facilitated the suture removal. She also supplied repeated doses of prophylactic antibiotics until she was satisfied that the wound was healing well enough not to be classified as highly vulnerable to infection.

I saw the same nurse practitioner whom the GP had booked me in with every week, and she was brilliant. She had this look about her that made you feel at ease. She spoke softly, and empathy oozed from her. I built a good rapport with her, and she learned of my story and how I ended up travelling abroad for surgery. I felt no judgement from her; she only offered words of compassion. Something the GP forgot about on my first visit was a core value of her profession.

The hole in my breast finally closed up after two long months, and I returned to my job on lighter duties in the school kitchen, where I still worked.

Let's talk about the architectural job done on my chest. Firstly, I know what you're probably wondering: *why did she not pay privately to do it in the UK?* Well, while it would have cost £7000 plus in the UK (at that point), it was only £1700 in Lithuania.

My nipples are odd and hard to convey to you. They had to be removed entirely, reshaped and put back on. This was because of the vast amount of breast tissue that was removed. They sit pretty high on my breasts, so low-cut tops and swimwear are sometimes a challenge. They have no sensation and are incapable of becoming erect. However, it's not such a bad thing now that I can wear tops suitable for going bra-less!

The incision scars go from my cleavage to being in line with my armpits.

There is what feels like loose skin at each breast's side. It's not an excessive amount, but it's hard to tone.

My post-operative bra was a 40DD, and I lived in it until it disintegrated from overuse; it didn't have a day off in a very long time.

...

In June of 2016, I turned twenty-one. I was very much overweight due to the lack of exercise and the volume of eating out of boredom as a consequence of my recovery.

I went on holiday with my best friend in August that year to celebrate my birthday. We had a brilliant time, and I felt free.

My best friend is a wise one; she knows everything. She told me when I began my relationship with my partner that we weren't right for each other.

She also knew him before we became an item, as she worked at the pub, too. She knew that we wouldn't work. But I didn't listen to her, and I stubbornly dived head-first into a full-on relationship where we lived together. I even became a stepmother. I spent a lot of time with his kids; they were great. That was also a hurdle in leaving.

Towards the end of our ten-day holiday, my best friend gave me a stern talking to. I love her brutal honesty.

Everyone needs a friend who will tell them when they are in the wrong or need a reality check.

"This is the first time that I've seen the real you in two years; you need to do something about this," she had said as we sat sipping cocktails at a bar near our hotel.

And so I did.

Chapter 3
Getting my Shit Together

Returning home from holiday was a nerve-wracking time. I had to come clean about my feelings for the man I had been living with for nearly two years now. I broke the news, and he sobbed and sobbed. So did I.

It broke my heart, but I knew that it was for the best. It wasn't because I was in love with him that it hurt; he was a good mate too if nothing else, and now I faced losing him. We had been friends before, and we sacrificed that friendship by becoming an item.

I drove to my mum's afterwards, and it felt like a weight had been lifted in one sense. However, I also felt guilty for leaving. It was the best decision for me and for him, and I had to remind myself of that.

I cried for hours as I sat on the bed in the room which had been mine before moving out. It was now bare with nothing of mine really in it; it didn't feel like it belonged to me anymore.

So, the next day, while he was at work, my mum and I got what was mine out of the house. I had messaged him to warn him I was doing it, just to make sure he wouldn't be in because I thought it would be easier if he was out of the house.

Some may think it was cowardly, but I did what I thought was best at the time.

It took two trips back and forth from my mum's to his house to gather everything, making the ordeal more stressful. It's not that I had vast amounts of stuff but a few oversized items meant that it wouldn't fit in one trip.

By the end of the day, my room was mine again; I felt much more settled and ready to start moving on with my life.

...

After the school summer holidays, I returned to work at the school kitchen; this was the next thing I had to tackle.

The people I worked with there were great but much older than me. There was one lady, about five years older than me, who I got on really well with. We spent the days chatting away the entire time.

I worked split shifts Monday to Friday, working 10:30 to 14:30 and then 17:00 to 19:00, all on minimum wage.

But I knew that I needed something that would offer me better opportunities and a greater salary. I began applying for jobs; I went for anything and everything that would grant me sufficient money and offered future prospects.

In early October, I had an interview for a mental health hospital that specialised in learning disabilities but had various other service users with complex needs, such as personality disorders. I was offered the job straightaway at the interview, and I eagerly accepted. It was something new, a change of direction, and better pay. It also provided training in different healthcare areas and aided me in becoming more confident in general.

...

Once I had resigned from the school kitchen and settled into my new role, the last task on my list was my weight.

I needed to figure out where to start; I knew little about what foods to eat and what workouts to do.

My friend had begun *Slimming World* two months before, and the fat seemed to be melting off her. So, my mum and I decided to give it a go.

Four months in, I had lost three stone!

It was an absolute game-changer for my confidence. I went from thirteen stone to ten without doing a single workout.

The weight loss, along with my much smaller breasts, had given me the confidence to wear clothes that I would never have imagined.

My entire look had changed.

I also progressively got blonder each time I went to the hairdresser and started using fake tan just for nights out. I began to actually care what I looked like again.

Working in my new job, I met many new friends and began socialising with them. There would often be a work night out every other week, and I would wear bodycon dresses and heels, something that, a year prior, didn't reside in my wardrobe.

I was finally happy with myself. I wouldn't say I was perfect but I was starting to like the person who I saw in the mirror.

Finally.

By this point, it had been a year since I had split up with my ex, and I was living my best life. The money I was earning was good, my friendship circle was expanding, my social life was busy, and my physical and mental health was thriving. I was more than content not being in a relationship, even though many of my friends were.

I worked an awful lot, maybe too much, but I was saving for two upcoming girls' getaways. Holiday clothes shopping this time round was an exciting prospect compared to the last trip, which I had loathed the idea of due to being overweight. Even though my breasts were smaller on the last holiday I had been on, I still didn't like what I saw in the mirror.

My friends and I went to Meadowhall (a shopping centre in Sheffield) which is an hour's drive from where we live. I bought loads! The only thing that I had struggled with was finding bikinis that came high enough on the cups to cover my highly-placed nipples.

Don't get me wrong, they aren't ridiculous to look at, but when it comes to bras and swimwear, my breasts are only just covered, and it makes me uncomfortable.

As I said before, I had two girls' holidays booked for the summer of 2017, and they were brilliant. They had been carefree and without worries.

When I had returned to normality after a summer of fun, life continued to be great and full of happiness. The holiday blues didn't hit me like they had before.

My *Slimming World* journey was still underway. Even though I was out most weekends drinking and eating a grease-filled pizza from the kebab shop at the end of the night, I was still happy with my progress. I was living my best life.

My monthly outgoings were car insurance, petrol, and rent for my mum and stepdad, so managing to save wasn't hard.

My relationship with my stepdad has always been good. When I was younger, there were some struggles when adjusting to life as a blended family, as he had two kids. It wasn't terrible in the slightest, but it wasn't totally smooth sailing either; however, we made it work. Our relationship is still good today, and both he and my mum live just around the corner from me. I love it.

Chapter 4
Prince Charming

At age seven, just two years before I began developing boulders on my chest, I joined a football team. We would play a match on Saturday mornings and train one night a week.

Back then, I was a beaming ginger with short, loose, curly hair and a very mischievous attitude to match.

I played the comedian in the group, just like I always have in every football, work team or friendship group throughout my life. My mum's dad (my grandad) and my uncle were exactly the same. The ability to make people laugh is a gene that runs in our family. I'd like to say my humour has completely changed since the age of seven and that I'm so much more mature at twenty-nine years old, but that's not the case. It has only become ruder.

Two of the girls that played were coaches' daughters, and they had a brother whom I used to refer to as 'fit'. They also had another brother who was quite a bit younger. I would often go to their house after a football match on the weekend and play on the trampoline, although the older brother's car garage was my favourite. It was no game plan for him to like me because I wasn't that clued up at seven years old. Plus, I looked like a little boy myself.

The girls' mum and brothers would come and watch us play our football matches and train most weeks. They were such a great family, much like my own.

Their mum and mine would stand chatting on the sidelines while our dads shouted at the players on the pitch. The older brother would kick a ball around, away from the pitch, in between watching the game.

As we got older, the age brackets for our football teams changed, and we were all split into separate ones.

One of the girls, who is only three months younger than me but in the year below me at school, joined the Lincoln City Centre of Excellence Football Club. Her sister, who is a year older, was put into the age bracket team above mine which their dad was still coaching.

As we were no longer playing together, we didn't spend any time together. But, when Facebook became a thing, I had the two sisters and the fit brother on my friends list; still, I never made contact.

We had a new coach for my team, with who my dad became mates, and he joined the coaching team as his second. I loved having my dad there but it did mean I couldn't mess around as much.

As my parents were separated, I used to only see him on weekends. But now that he was part of the coaching team, he would attend the midweek training sessions, and I thought it was great.

I played football until around age fifteen, when the dreaded space hoppers attached to my chest bounced me off the pitch.

Later, on the 22nd of December 2017, I was twenty-two. It was three days before Christmas and it turned out to really be the most magical time of them all.

I had arranged to meet my best friend that night, *the wise one*, for a Christmas drink. It wasn't planned to be anything crazy, just a civilised social drink. I was wearing a jumper, skinny jeans, winter boots and a puffy coat. We met at a pub in a posh area of Lincoln, which is only a five-minute walk into the city centre.

A few bottles of prosecco later, some more friends we had bumped into joined us. The atmosphere was great; everyone was in the Christmas spirit, and we played drinking games.

After sinking a lot more drinks, we headed for the clubs. By this point, we were all very drunk, and I could imagine our dancing was like watching Mr Bean running on an ice rink.

A group of guys came over and chatted with us. I knew a few of them, and so did my friends. However, there was one I recognised who had exceptionally spectacular dance moves that matched my vibe. It was the fit brother, Jake.

He was just as gorgeous as I remembered him to be.

"I know you," I said.

What a chat-up line!

He replied, "I know you too."

So far, so good; he remembered me.

He bought me a drink, and we danced and chatted about all kinds of drunken nonsense.

I completely forgot about my friends, and to be honest, I completely forgot about the rest of the human race.

He also deserted his mates, and we got lost in conversation.

My friends came over and said that they were going to another club. We also went with them and walked ahead, totally engrossed by each other's personalities.

We laughed and joked; I think I had fallen in love approximately thirty seconds after bumping into him.

When we got into the next club, we were still glued to each other's sides as we headed for the bar. While in the queue for a drink, we ended up kissing each other's faces off.

He asked me, "Are you coming home with me?"

Even though I had never gone home with anyone from a night out, I did not hesitate to say, "Yes!"

OH MY GOD!

It had also been a while since I had been intimate with a guy; I felt ready but I also couldn't believe my luck!

We then abandoned the drinks queue and our friends and went to get a taxi. I don't need to explain what happened; I think you can guess.

I woke up in his bed in the morning, and my first thought was: *This used to be the playroom. I wonder if he still has his garage?*

However, I didn't ask him that question.

As I turned over, he was awake and just as gorgeous as I had thought he was the night before. He kissed me, and all I could think was to not breathe on him because he might die due to my awful alcohol-stained breath.

We lay in bed, and the conversation flowed as much as it had when we bumped into each other the night before.

Eventually, I decided that I needed to see what I looked like, but he had no mirror in his room. I needed the bathroom, too, but his room was downstairs, and I could hear people up and about.

Brilliant.

I got dressed and planned to make a run for it.

I quickly made my way down the hallway to the bathroom and made it outside the door without anyone seeing me.

Phew!

I went to open the door, but it began opening from the other side, making me jump, and I trumped— loudly. It was so embarrassing.

It was the older one of the sisters coming out of the bathroom.

"Oh, hello, lovely! Long time no see," she said.

I laughed and replied, "Morning," in what felt to be a high-pitched voice. *God knows where that came from.* Also, I wasn't sure if she had heard me trump just a few moments ago, but I wanted the ground to swallow me up.

Once we passed each other in the doorway and I made it inside the bathroom, I locked the door and tried to calm myself down after that humiliating encounter I had just experienced with his sister.

I looked in the mirror, and I could only describe my look as resembling the character Beetlejuice. Around my eyes were dark marks from smudged mascara, and my hair was one big knotty blonde mess— *what a catch.*

I sorted myself out and went back to Jake's room.
He asked if I wanted a drink, and I desperately needed one due to my dehydrated state from last night's prosecco, so we went into the kitchen where all his family was.

Great. What a time for a reunion.

They all remembered me and were as great as I had remembered them to be. His mum asked me if I would like some breakfast as she was cooking eggs and bacon.

I said, "Yes, please; I'll take everything."

Hungover and hungry!

We ate breakfast and chatted with his sisters and mum; his younger brother was also there. Before I left, his dad returned from work and said, "Oh good, the ginger is back."

His dad still had shit jokes then, I take it?

Even though I was blonde at the time and hadn't seen him for over ten years, he recognised me immediately. *He* hadn't changed a bit. I laughed and just said hello.

My mum texted me to see if I was okay because, obviously, I hadn't made it home the night before.

Me:
You'll never believe whose bed I woke up in! Be home soon.

Mum:
I'm not sure I really want to know, haha.

Jake took me home after breakfast in his lady killer one series black BMW with tinted windows. I was already thinking about asking him if I could take it for a spin.

I only lived in a village nearby, and the journey took just under a ten-minute drive from his house. When we pulled up outside my house, he leaned over and kissed me goodbye. I did my best to play it cool, but all that I wanted was to squeal with giddiness.

I walked down the driveway towards my house, smiling like the Cheshire Cat.

I shouted hello when I walked through the door, and Mum's voice replied from the kitchen. I walked in, sat at the table while she was pottering, and told her everything. But I left out the gory details.

I have always told my mum far too much, but she's also my mate, so she has to put up with it.

She had remembered Jake's family from my early football days and commented how lovely she recalled them to be.

I took a shower and was still on cloud nine. I then went to bed for a few hours, realising that I hadn't slept much the night before.

I woke up to Jake's message on Facebook Messenger and became all giddy and flushed. He was only asking how I was, but at this point, I was already planning our wedding.

We were messaging each other continuously.

Like I said, it had been ages since I had been intimate with a guy.

My friends, who I abandoned the night before, knew of my recently unplanned celibacy issues, and they were eagerly messaging me for the update. I had just slept with my future husband, girls, that's all.

I dropped my mum and my stepdad in town later that afternoon. They were out socialising for their Christmas drinks. I was also going out that night with my work friends for our Christmas piss-up, but it was too early to start getting ready.

So, I had the house to myself, and I thought: *fuck it, I'll ask the fit brother, sorry, Jake, to come over.*

At first, he said that he couldn't. He had some family at his house.

Me:
No worries. I've just taken my mum and stepdad into town, so I've got the house for myself.

I crawled back into bed after sending that message in an attempt to get a little more sleep before another night on the booze.

I looked at my phone after a few minutes of being in bed.

Jake:
Be there in 10.

He had sent it five minutes ago! *SHIT!* I immediately thought that I should put some makeup on. But there wasn't any time; I didn't expect him to be so quick.

He came over, and I answered the door, acting cool as a cucumber in my polar bear onesie with naturally dried hair and a bare face. My enticing look worked a treat, and we 'cuddled' twice.

The laughing and joking from before was still in full swing. We just *clicked*.

Once he had gone, I updated the girls in the group chat and started getting ready for my night out with my work friends while messaging Jake.

My friend came over to get ready, and she stayed at my house that night. I divulged the last twenty-four hours to her and couldn't stop smiling.

She had said, "I hope you're going to clean-sheet your bed before I stay in it tonight!"

Haha, I had forgotten to do that.

We were drinking prosecco and singing while getting ready; I was absolutely buzzing. We got a taxi into town and went to the bar where we met up with our work colleagues. I eagerly updated them all about my new love match and husband-to-be, not becoming tired of talking about him one bit.

Being the comedian that I am, I joked about changing my last name on Facebook to his, which my friends obviously encouraged.

However, I was joking and had to hide my phone from them all night to stop them from hacking my social media and scaring him away.

Jake and I continued texting constantly during the Christmas period until we met up again between Christmas and New Year's. And that was it. We couldn't stay away from each other. I had nearly chosen my wedding dress at this point. *I joke! Sort of.*

We became an item pretty soon after, and my world felt like the most perfect place to be. Jake is the nicest, most laid-back, easygoing, loving, and trusting person that I've ever met. He will do anything for anyone.

I felt like the luckiest girl on the planet. *I still do.*

Six months into our relationship, we decided to open Jake a *Help to Buy ISA*. I already had one in place, as my mum had encouraged me to set one up when I began earning a decent wage. We weren't looking for a home to buy together that early on, but we just figured that it was a smart move.

We went on our first holiday abroad together in the summer of 2018, and I was just so in love that it was unreal. Nothing has changed on that front.

However, from all the dates we went on and films, we would binge eat chocolate and sweets, too, and my weight crept up again.

I attempted *Slimming World* again after the summer, but for some reason, it didn't work as well as it had done before.

...

In November 2018, I began a new job in a pharmacy. It had better social hours and no weekend work, so seeing Jake was always easy. After two years of working in the mental health hospital, I was ready for a change.

I began working at the pharmacy as a Medicine Counter Assistant and loved it. It also offered more progression, which I had exhausted in my previous role. However, what I had obtained from my former job was various training and the national care certificate which did come in handy later on.

There was also no threat of violence like there was at the mental health hospital, and going to work felt relaxed. However, we did get some lively characters coming in for their methadone who could behave quite antisocial if they didn't have an in-date prescription.

Everything had fallen into place.

Chapter 5
A Year to Remember

I needed to approach my weight with a different solution. Although my 2019 New Year's resolution to lose weight was cliché, I desperately wanted to stick to it as we were planning to go to Florida with Jake's family later that year. I didn't want to be self-conscious in a bikini.

Jake was a boxer back then, extremely physically fit and in good shape. He still is, but he no longer does boxing. He has one of those lucky body types where he eats what he wants and doesn't put on a pound.

I asked for his guidance, and he used his knowledge of nutrition to teach me about macros: fats, proteins, and carbohydrates.

He put me on a balanced diet and a 1500-calorie deficit; he even taught me the science behind it.

It's not that he ever complained about my weight gain; he knew that it was a hurdle for me and that I wanted to overcome it. As normal, he was only being supportive and caring.

I began running, something that I said I would do once I had smaller breasts but never did until nearly three years later. At first, it was disgustingly brutal. I had to really push myself to do it, and Jake would come with me, giving me the encouragement I needed. I went from only being able to run half a mile to four in a couple of months.

From the start of 2019 to the end of March that year, I had lost a stone and a half.

I can't say that I was consistently strict with my food and drink intake on weekends, but my body was a temple from Monday to Friday. This is probably not an advised plan by the experts in the fitness industry but I love prosecco and chocolate too much! *Guilty pleasures.*

...

While working at the pharmacy, I became close to one of the women there. However, the other colleagues told me that she was a tough nut to crack at first and standoffish when it came to newbies.

A few months in, we were joined at the hip at work, much to everyone's shock.

She was also a workout fanatic, something that I was slowly becoming. We built a friendship on humour and fitness. She was already a member at the local gym which was not even a five-minute drive from the pharmacy. I joined the same one, and we worked out together during our lunch hour.

We would get there at precisely 13:04, work out, be in the shower by 13:40, leave the gym at 13:52, and be back at the pharmacy at 14:00; we were both sticklers for routine.

We still talk all the time now and meet up about twice a year for bottomless brunch instead of a workout.

I sometimes ran in the mornings before my work day began at the pharmacy. I would then do a HIIT (high-intensity interval training) at lunchtime at the gym; the weight continued to melt off.

...

In early March 2019, I noticed a lump in my left breast. I had felt it when I laid in the bath, washing my body. Its position matched that of the scarring from the anchor point following surgery. I tried not to panic and said to myself that it was just scar tissue and was probably only more prominent now because I had lost weight.

I went to the GP and they believed that the area I was worried about on my breast was scar tissue. However, they seemed to be more concerned about the hard mass situated to the side of my left breast. I had known that it was there but I just thought that it had healed that way with being the 'problem' breast.

It never caused me any pain, just a dull sensation that made me wince more than anything if it was touched. Jake learnt quickly that squeezing that one was off-limits.

The GP advised me that they wanted to refer me to the breast clinic for further investigation.

I left thinking, "What the hell could that be?"

I had asked the doctor while I was there if she thought it was cancerous.

She replied, "I don't believe so but it's hard to say."

A few days later, a letter came through the post with an appointment date scheduled for two weeks' time. I was anxious for the next couple of weeks. I couldn't help but start resenting breasts altogether; they were causing me problems again! When would it end?

When the day of my appointment arrived, I was so nervous. Jake came with me, and I was so thankful that he had, even if it was just to hold my hand for reassurance.

I was called in to see the consultant; he examined my chest and told me that he didn't believe this to be a problem, but to make sure, he wanted me to have an ultrasound scan.

I then had to return to the waiting room to be called in for it.

I was called in not long after and I remember laying on the bed with tears just falling down my face; I had thought that my breast issues were over. She did the scan and seemed pretty certain that the hard mass was just an accumulated fat lump from healing; I think that's how she explained it anyway.

She also took a biopsy of the area, which wasn't the nicest experience. Then, she sent me to reception to book an appointment for a couple of weeks after the results were back.

Another anxious wait.

Although I did feel more reassured after the clinic appointment and the professionals were not too concerned with their findings, I was still apprehensively waiting for the confirmed result.

The day came. Jake, again, came with me.

We sat in the waiting room, just like before, and I could feel my palms beginning to sweat; it was worse than Eminem's palms in 8 Mile.

I heard my name called and squeezed Jake's hand a little tighter.

Once we were in the room with the consultant, he got to the point straight away. No cancerous cells were found!

Phew!

However, I was given instructions to be extra vigilant when self-checking my breasts for lumps in future.

...

My role at the pharmacy quickly exhausted itself for me. Not long into my new role, I was already helping with the dispensing area between customers coming in.

I started to learn about myself then. For example, I now knew that I loved a challenge when it came to my work life. A staff member left her role in the dispensary and I filled it straightaway, much like they did with my role on the counter.

More responsibility, more challenge; I loved it.

I began assembling patients' weekly medicine boxes which entailed remembering to order their medication every four weeks, sending them out for delivery on time and putting the medication in the correct time slot. It also required a lot of concentration and I would often come home feeling drained after a day of assembling the boxes.

By May 2019, our *Help to Buy ISA*s had been running for nearly a year. We also had another savings account that we began to put money into a few months back and quickly accumulated a deposit-worthy amount.

We wanted to stay in the same village that Jake was already living in. It's such a lovely, quiet area with a few shops, takeaways, two pubs, and two schools.

The location is also perfect for getting into town quickly.

What more could you ask for?

While we were out walking one time, we saw a house that was up for sale. As soon as we got home, we had a look on *Rightmove.co.uk* at the house we had just seen. This had sparked something in us and it was time to start seriously looking.

The following week, we arranged to see the house and another that we had seen on the internet that was in the same village.

Our first viewing was of the house that we had seen on the walk. Jake's parents and my mum came with us which was great as they noticed things that we didn't and asked the estate agent questions we would have never thought of.

That house was a 'no-go' due to its smaller size and a lot needed to be done to build a family there.

Our viewing of the next house was a few days later. Again, the parents came with us and we felt more comfortable asking questions and inspecting the areas from our trial at the previous property.

It hadn't been lived in for the previous two years as it had belonged to an elderly lady who had moved into a care home and passed away. She had no immediate family, and her house was left to her nephew, who lived on the other side of the country.

The garden was overgrown and the inside had a fusty smell, with woodchip wallpaper and green pattern carpets. But, despite these aesthetic issues, we loved it.

This was the one.

It needed a lot of work but it had the space, both indoors and outdoors, to become a perfect family home.

We put an offer in later that day. It was below the asking price, but if you don't ask, you don't get, right? However, our offer was rejected, and we were told that others were interested. So, we came back with another offer. Again, it was denied, but the estate agent said to us that we were in a great position as first-time buyers with no chain.

What felt like a game of tennis, with our offers competing with those of the other buyer, eventually turned into sudden death.

We were given a date in July 2019 and a noon deadline to submit our best and final offers; it was so nerve-wracking.

I had been at work at the pharmacy, unable to concentrate on preparing medication boxes because I was eagerly looking at the clock in anticipation.

We had been deciding whether to go beyond or stick to the asking price because of our good position. In the end, I left Jake with the final decision because I just had no idea. It was a total gamble.

The clock ticked one minute past the deadline and I eagerly awaited to hear from Jake who was negotiating.

Five past noon and still nothing!

I am impatient anyway, so this felt like a level of urgency that was all too much for my nerves. I just needed to *know*.

Twenty minutes after the deadline, I finally got a text from Jake. He said, very simply, "We got it."

Erm... WHAT!?

I screamed with excitement and happiness. I rang him straight away, not quite believing his text and needing to hear him say it.

We were over the moon and in complete shock that we were growing up and going to become homeowners.

Jake, being the superstar man he is, dealt with all of the paperwork side of things. Death by admin! It was one of the worst things ever for me, and it still is. I cannot stand writing emails, waiting in telephone call queues to speak to someone, and generally giving my time towards it. We didn't even need to delegate roles; it just happened naturally.

In August 2019, when we went to Florida, poor Jake, the admin man, was attending to emails in between rides at Disney World. That was a holiday like no other. Before going, I had thought that it would be just for kids but how wrong was I? It is the most magical place on earth and the most exciting place to be at *any* age.

We also booked park tickets for Universal Studios, which was absolutely incredible! Their Harry Potter section had a Hogwarts that looked more like a Hogwarts than, well, Hogwarts!

At this point, I was 9st 2lbs, the lightest that I've been since I think I was about five years old. I was also two and a half stone down since I began my cliché New Year's resolution.

Life was good.

Chapter 6
When the World Turned Upside Down

On October 14th 2019, we finally opened the door to our new two-bedroom dormer bungalow after what felt like forever waiting.

Jake had gotten the call mid-morning to collect the keys, and we eagerly drove into town to the estate agents to collect them.

Jake and his dad began work straightaway, pulling the upstairs ceilings down while our mums and I were downstairs, steaming and then peeling the dreaded woodchip paper off the walls.

One Friday evening, Jake and his dad needed to get some supplies for the building work. They left his mum and me to finish pulling wallpaper off in the living room before they could start their DIY there.

They came back after just over an hour with a chippy-tea and their supplies; they found us in a mess. We were so drunk. When Jake and his dad were out, I nipped to the local shop and bought two bottles of prosecco. We sipped them, not doing any of the work we had been left with. They weren't shocked by our behaviour.

Jake's mum and I have a fantastic relationship but sometimes, we aren't good influences on each other when it comes to alcohol.

My mum and Jake's sister (the eldest of the two) are also just as bad; they are easily led. My sister and Jake's youngest sister don't have this weak trait like the rest of us and aren't simply swayed by someone asking if they want a glass.

Work had been non-stop on our new house for a solid two months. The bathroom had been ripped out and replaced with a lovely brand new one with dark tiled walls, a waterfall shower, a P-shaped bath and a new sink unit.

An arched wall had separated the kitchen from the dining room. It was knocked out and made open-plan, with a hell of a colour change done on the walls and bright white tiled flooring put down.

The upstairs ceilings were ripped out and had been reinsulated too.

Everywhere had been plastered with new carpets and paint jobs.

We filled the house with furniture and, two weeks before Christmas 2019, we could finally move in.

Soon after, we rescued a cat. Jake took a lot of convincing but I loved them. I have always had cats at home with my mum and wanted one of my own. He finally caved, and we went to visit a local cat rescue charity. There, we found our little fur baby, Pumba, the only name we could agree on. She is not so little anymore and is actually quite chubby now.

...

In February 2020, I received a letter through the post; it was my first smear screening appointment! Not every woman looks forward to this and the thought of it made me cringe.

Maybe it's the word 'smear'; it sounds cringe to me, despite how vital they are.

I attended the appointment and had the test done. Then, I had to wait a few weeks for my results and they came back HPV-positive.

For God's sake!

Of course, panic set in and I thought the worst... *I'm going to get cervical cancer and die— end of.*

I was instructed to go back the following year to have another smear due to the result to see if it had gone. A year feels like a long time to know if a virus in your body has turned into cancer!

I tell you, being a woman is complicated, bloody work.

...

Soon after, the world went into turmoil. COVID-19 had begun to attack the human race, and everyone started to live in fear.

In early March 2020, I had just begun my dispensing apprenticeship course to get the qualification for the job I was already doing but not getting paid for. I had a time frame of one year to eighteen months to complete it. The course was demanding and I was required to have at least one day where I could sit at work in the staff room and complete the required modules. There were deadlines to meet and the work was very in-depth.

Swiftly following the start of my course, the virus became more prominent in the UK and, soon after, the country went into lockdown.

Key workers were the only ones allowed to continue working and, being in medicine, I was one of them.

Work became a strange place to walk into. Customers and colleagues wore masks and were extra cautious, and social distancing measures were hard to maintain in a small pharmacy. To make it more difficult, there was no gym at lunchtime to escape to anymore.

Some colleagues had to leave due to vulnerability and some were suffering mentally from what was happening to the world; they took sick. This meant that the workload began to pile up for those of us who were left. We had to stretch ourselves thin to facilitate the purpose of the pharmacy's services and I took on every patient with a medication tray because the lady who also did them was off work for the foreseeable.

The apprenticeship I had started not long before was taking a backseat. But, my online tutor understood.

It was soon July. After a few months of constantly being overworked, I began to crumble.

One day, after driving back to work from being at home during my lunch hour, I had an emotional breakdown when I parked up. I couldn't get out of the car and I couldn't catch my breath.

I felt so overwhelmed by everything that I began to dream about my ever-expanding job list in my sleep.

After my breakdown in the car, I spoke with Jake about reducing my hours from full-time. He agreed that it would be the best move to help reduce my apprehension about work. No one knew how long the effects of the pandemic were going to last so the uncertainty of how long I had to cope with work stressors was unknown; my anxiety was through the roof.

I only reduced my hours by one afternoon, but psychologically, it helped to see it as four and a half days of work compared to a full five. The area manager decided that he would employ an extra pair of hands, too, but it took a while for them to get settled and trained to work in a dispensary.

My workload had reduced but only minimally. And, I can't say I felt a whole lot of stress relief.

Back in April 2020, I also started having trouble with my contraception pill. I was on the mini pill that you take every day with no breaks or periods. I began to have breakthrough bleeds and the GP told me that it was normal after being on it for so long. The bleeding became more frequent and I persisted with it until early August 2020 when we decided that I should come off the pill. Mainly, it was because of the issues I was having but we also weren't totally against falling pregnant either.

At the beginning of September 2020, my first period came; it was exactly four weeks after finishing the pill. *Clockwork.*

Pregnancy hadn't even crossed our minds as a possibility straight away as we thought it would take months after being on the pill so long.

The UK was dipping in and out of lockdown; no one knew whether they were coming or going. Work stressors were still prominent, and I thought that those were probably the cause of my female health problems that began in the April.

October 12th, 2020. What a day that was. It was a Monday; I had woken up to do a workout at 06:00 with Jake's mum at her house since it was only around the corner from ours. She is also into fitness, and, throughout lockdown, we were in the so-called 'bubbles'; we were allowed to interact and continue working out together in her garage, where she had a proper boxing punch bag and various weighted equipment.

The workout that morning was hard. I had felt so tired and drained. My lower abdomen felt slightly crampy and I couldn't keep up with Jake's mum and sister who had joined in that morning. Usually, I get told that I'm a beast and just keep going.

I got home and had a shower. I felt horrendous by this point and I thought that it was my period coming as it was late. I had put that down to my body adjusting from the effects of contraception.

Once I had gotten out of the shower, I went upstairs to get ready for work, but I just couldn't do it. I had no energy, and I looked as white as a ghost.

This must be a horrendous period coming, was all I could think.

I decided to call in sick to work; I wouldn't have been able to give the level of concentration that my job required that day.

Jake had already left for work when I returned from my poorly-performed workout. I texted him and told him that I was feeling shit and that I had called in sick to work. He had asked me if I thought I could be pregnant.

Surely not?

There was one pregnancy test left over from a pack in our bathroom cabinet; we'd bought it during a scare we had earlier that year, probably around the time I started bleeding on the pill.

I did the test.

FUCK!

There was a second line; it wasn't the boldest but it was prominent enough to see. I still didn't believe it. I rang Jake and told him what had happened but also that I wasn't certain.

I sent my mum a photo of the test too and she couldn't believe it.

Mum:
Do another one!

I decided to wait for Jake to get home from work to go to Tesco and get a digital one. *Is the most impatient woman in the world being patient at a time like this?* But I needed to see it in writing to believe it. That was the LONGEST day of my life. Waiting for him to come home had felt like a week, but it was only six hours. *Jesus, Jake, hurry up!*

As soon as he was home and had changed, we headed to Tesco.

When we arrived home, I still lacked energy and just felt off. I did the test as soon as we walked through the door; I hadn't even taken my coat off.

The anticipation of the wait was breaking us.

We were looking away and then would glance back at the test repeatedly. Then, eventually, the result appeared: pregnant.

HOLY FUCK.

We hugged each other with happiness and shock. When we looked at each other, we both had glossy eyes; we were ecstatic.

My mum was shielding due to COVID-19 to protect my vulnerable grandparents and my dad lives on the other side of the city and was at work. So, instead of seeing them in person, I sent my mum a photo of the test; she was over the moon. I also phoned my dad; he was so happy to hear the news.

Jake's parents made it well known that they were excited for grandkids. It wasn't just directed at Jake and me; it was directed towards all of their children. Jake couldn't wait to tell his mum and dad. Living around the corner from us and being in our 'bubble', we headed to his their house. However, the pain was still lingering but I just kept brushing it off. I had never been pregnant before so I didn't know what I was supposed to be feeling.

When we arrived at Jake's parents' house, all his siblings were there too. *Perfect!* Telling them all at the same time would be amazing, even though I had mentioned our possible news to his youngest sister earlier in the day when we were messaging, like we often do.

When we walked into his parents' kitchen, everyone was in there. Their kitchen is open-plan and links to the conservatory and dining area which is where we all usually hang out together.

His mum was cooking and Jake put the pregnancy test on the kitchen worktop.

Her face was a picture. "No!" she said in shock, squealing and hugging us both. Everyone else came in to see what was going on and they saw the test; everyone was over the moon. It was the best day.

I couldn't believe it: we were having a baby!

I rang the doctors to get an appointment with the midwife to book the pregnancy. It was a good few weeks away, as it happens at eight weeks of gestation.

A couple of days after, his mum gave me a package. It was a navy jumper with the word "MAMA" written on the front in leopard print; my favourite pattern.

The person that I was most worried about telling was my sister. She had recently been going through tests for her fertility as she had been having issues with her menstrual cycle. She was diagnosed with polycystic ovary syndrome (PCOS).

Little did she know that, while she was sitting at her diagnosis appointment, she was pregnant. Not long after, she was at work but she began to bleed heavily and collapsed. She was rushed to hospital, still not knowing that she was with child, and was rushed into surgery. The outcome was that her unknown pregnancy was discovered to be ectopic.

She woke up post-surgery to be told all of this information and that she had lost a fallopian tube.

Can you imagine the heartbreak? What a mind-fuck.

My poor sister had to go through that physical and mental struggle. Four years on and she still is.

She was happy for me about my own news but I can imagine it broke her heart.

...

On Tuesday the 28th of October 2020, I was at work and felt my world shatter. The cramping pain I had been experiencing just two weeks prior was worse. It had lingered around since the day before we found out we were pregnant. I was standing at the computer desk when it felt like I had come on my period.

I rushed to the toilet and there was blood. Not a lot and it was old; but it was there.

I panicked and was sent home from work. I rang Jake and told him what was happening, and he came home from work earlier that day. I also phoned the GP, who made a referral to the *Lincoln Early Pregnancy Assessment Unit* (EPAU).

People I spoke to told me not to worry and that it might not be anything but I knew. I knew that I was losing what was going to be my 'baby'; inverted commas because, medically, it wasn't yet classed as a fetus.

By the end of the working day, I still had not heard from the EPAU.

We had already booked a private early pregnancy scan that was due to happen the following week. She was lovely when I spoke to her on the phone to book only a week before what was happening now. I sat on the sofa at home, tormenting myself by asking Google questions. I just needed to know what was happening. I decided to phone her again for some advice, and she offered me her earliest appointment in two days to see what was going on if EPAU hadn't been in touch.

That night, I went to bed. The blood wasn't more than spotting but I thought I had best put a sanitary towel on. And I was right to do so.

I woke up the following day to what was like a really heavy period and the cramping pains to go with it. I rang my mum and she came round.

She sat with me and Jake while we sobbed and she messaged her midwife friend for advice. My mum was already in an emotional phase from what my sister had just gone through; it must have been hard on her.

I remember going to the toilet to change my sanitary towel, and I knew that I had just passed what was to be my 'baby'. I felt it. I felt my heartbreak. I caught it on some tissue because I wanted to look at it and inspect it. It sounds gross, I know.

My mum had called 111 for advice as we still hadn't heard from EPAU. They made an appointment for me at the *Urgent Treatment Centre* (UTC) and told me to take what I believed to be my future baby with me. Jake and I got changed out of our pyjamas and headed for the UTC.

I sat in the waiting room, staring at this bit of Blu Tack on the wall that had nothing stuck to it. I wondered what notice it had held before it became redundant. In that moment, I felt like that bit of Blu Tac.

Jake wasn't allowed in with me due to COVID-19 policies at the hospital. That was hard.

I must have looked like a zombie sitting there, staring at the wall with my little bathroom waste bag, holding the blood-stained blob that was going to be my baby inside, wrapped in a bit of tissue.

They called my name, and I went in with my little bag.

The woman attending to me was doing my clinical observations and wasn't the doctor I was due to see. She couldn't have been less empathetic if she tried. She showed no compassion, regardless of the tears falling down my face.

After that, I had to return to the waiting room and wait for the doctor to see me. I went in when my name was called and answered his questions. He was very stern and to the point. It's not really the kind of personality you want to be dealing with when you are miscarrying.

He had asked me how I knew that I was experiencing this. I explained everything and then he had said, "That doesn't mean you have *lost* the baby."

I told him that I had what I thought was the embryo come out of me in my little plastic bag.

"I do not need to see," he had said.

He informed me that he was going to make an appointment at EPAU. I told him that the GP had said he was doing that yesterday but I still haven't heard from them.

"Wait," was his reply.

Yeah, thanks.

I went to the car park where Jake was waiting for me and we went home none the wiser. The whole thing had felt like a complete waste of time.

We still hadn't heard from EPAU by the following day so we attended the private scan first thing. She was brilliant with us; precisely the sort of personality you want to deal with through a miscarriage.

She internally scanned me and confirmed that we'd had a miscarriage. Finally, an answer. Not that we didn't already know but we needed to have professional confirmation.

About five minutes after leaving the private scan, my phone rang. It was EPAU. They apologised for the long wait and said that they wanted to see me later that day.

I told them that I had just been to see a private sonographer who had confirmed my miscarriage. However, they told me that it was important that NHS services saw me and they booked me for an appointment at another hospital in the trust that had the capacity to see me... an hour away!

We just wanted the ordeal over so we went.

Another internal, uncomfortable scan later they confirmed what we had been told earlier that day. They did a pregnancy test on me, which was negative, and told me to do another at the end of the following week. If it was positive, we were to call back. They also gave us a memory box too which meant a lot to us, and we still have it today.

We came home and buried the little plastic bag with our embryo inside and the positive digital pregnancy test too— o*ur baby.* We then put a flower on top that we had bought from the garden centre on the way back especially.

The next few days, I was broken. My heart hurt and I felt empty. So did Jake. I just wanted to be pregnant again. It was the most emotional pain that I have ever experienced.

It made me think of how much my sister's experience must have hurt her. How had she coped? How does anyone cope with this?

I had a newfound respect for her. What she must have felt and still would be feeling was probably close to hell. Complete mental and emotional hell.

After I finished bleeding, the next week, I went back to work. Normality felt like it had to resume.

We began being intimate again. It wasn't advised but we both knew that it was what we wanted after being so happy to find out we were pregnant. And, when it was taken from us, it made us want it that bit more.

For the next three weeks, I was still tearful on most days. I would sit on the sofa at night to relax after a demanding day's work and the tears would just come. Jake would hold me in an attempt to console me; it sometimes worked and sometimes it didn't.

Four weeks following the miscarriage, I was expecting to have my period.

It didn't come.

Chapter 7
After Every Storm comes the Rainbow

Sunday November 22nd 2020. My mum and stepdad had just moved into their new house a few days earlier which was to be a renovation project just around the corner of our house. It was early morning, probably around 07:30. I was sitting in my bathroom, about to get ready for a day of visiting.

We were going to my mum's new house as my stepsister had just had a baby and was bringing him to see my mum, stepdad, Jake and me. Then, we were going to Jake's mum's home for a roast dinner, like we do every Sunday.

As I sat there, I was looking at the bathroom cabinet, knowing that there was a pregnancy test sitting in there waiting for me, calling out to me. I don't know why I bought it, really, but I did when I bought the other test to confirm we were no longer displaying a positive pregnancy status after the miscarriage.

I had no actual date of when my period was due but if we went from the dates I had last bled with the miscarriage, it was just around the corner.

Shall I do it?

I worked it out, and I was three days off my expected self-calculated period (give or take). A little voice in my head shouted at me: *just do it!*

What's the worst that can happen?

Fuck it.

I got the test out from the cabinet and used it.

I sat there staring at it afterwards. I hadn't gotten off the toilet; I was just waiting for the result. *Come on, come on, come on!*

It was one of those Clear Blue early tests that give another singular line if you're pregnant. When I looked at it, there was only one line. *Oh well.*

To be honest, I don't really know what I was expecting.

I put the test on the side of the bathroom sink, got up from the toilet, and washed my hands. I turned on the shower and the extractor fan, which requires the light to be on for it to work. I flicked it on and was about to get in the shower when I glanced at the test again.

I thought my eyes were tricking me.

Was that another line?

Surely not?

I stood looking at the test for what felt like ages. It was like time had stood still. I didn't blink for at least a minute; this is a slight exaggeration but you get the picture.

It was the faintest line, but it was there; I could see it!

"JAKE!" I shouted. "WAKE UP!"

He came rushing downstairs, probably expecting to find me trembling away from a spider (which is usually what he finds when I shout his name with urgency).

"What, what, what?!" he replied.

He burst into the bathroom like the hero spider-catcher he is to find me in complete shock, looking down at a white plastic stick.

"Look!" I said. "We are pregnant!"

At first, he was confused and in shock. He couldn't believe it. It was like he no longer understood the English language.

"What… I don't understand. *What?*"

We decided to get another digital one like we had before to see it in writing; we were both in disbelief and sceptical that it might just be from the hormones from the last time.

But I had done a pregnancy test following the miscarriage as advised and that was a definite negative; I saw it. It read 'Not pregnant', just like the test that EPAU had done on me following the miscarriage.

As it was Sunday, we had to wait until 10 am to buy the test from Tesco. *How inconvenient.*

We got showered and dressed and patiently waited about an hour at home until we could go.

Once purchased, we drove home, and I did the test immediately. *Deja vu.* And, like before, I hadn't taken my coat off when I peed on the stick; my impatience was getting the better of me.

We stood waiting for the result to show. It felt like a much longer wait than the first time we had done this! *Tick tock.*

Soon, it was there, the word we had been waiting for. The word we so desperately wanted to see: Pregnant...

I'm pregnant...
I'M PREGNANT!
Sounds of joy left both of our mouths.

We were beyond shocked and over the moon. I suddenly didn't feel sad anymore. I hadn't instantly forgotten what we had just been through. But it was like the fire had been put back into my heart after it had been blown out.

We couldn't wait. We needed to tell our families.

I needed to tell our families.

I don't judge anyone on their choice of how or when they announce their pregnancies; each to their own. For me, I'm glad I told them straight away, both times. It made the emotional support that bit stronger for Jake and me when we lost our first pregnancy; we needed that. And it helped them understand the anxieties that we would obviously have around this pregnancy.

My mum was the first to hear the news, shortly after we walked through her front door. She had been in total disbelief, shock, confusion and happiness. She was also worried that it was a crossover of hormones from the last pregnancy too.

Still, I explained to her that we already had confirmation that there were no pregnancy hormones from the test we did and the one at EPAU. Of course, the thought had popped into my head: *what if they were false negatives?* But it seemed a bit extreme to have two faulty tests.

I just knew. I knew in my heart and I knew in my gut. This was it.

We then went to Jake's parents, who live just around the corner from my mum. I hadn't had the chance to wear the "MAMA" top that his mum had bought me when we were pregnant the first time so I decided to wear it; *why not?*

We walked in and his mum was just in the kitchen, pottering around.

She looked at me to say hi but pulled a face of concern more than anything when she saw my top. She tried not to make it obvious but she couldn't hide it from me as I watched her every move, waiting for it to sink in.

She hadn't said anything about it and had begun to talk about a different topic of conversation.

Jake said, "Mum, have you seen Jazz's top?" She looked at us both, confused and shocked, not knowing what to say. Jake just replied to her expression with a big smile whilst nodding.

"OH MY GOD!" she said. She hugged us, but, just like my mum, she still had concerns as we had fallen pregnant again so quickly.

I had tried to reassure both of our mums the best that I could but they just felt like, as it was so close to the other pregnancy, the hormones might still be lingering around.

It was not that they were putting a downer on our news; it was just a motherly concern. I would be the same.

That day, I bought another test. It was a Clear Blue *'How many weeks'* indicator test. It came back with the result of *'1-2 weeks pregnant'*.

The week after, I did the same style test again and it said *'2-3 weeks pregnant'*.

That seemed to have put their concerns, *and mine,* more at bay. We decided to book an early scan at six weeks with the same woman who gave the answers when we miscarried.

...

Things at work were still full on. My workload was still the same amount, if not more.

During May and June 2020, we tried to limit the number of patients who wanted a medication box. We also attempted to get patients already on the medication box service to revert back to the typical way of ordering and taking their medication. We never denied those who needed them for reasons such as having a brain impairment, feeling overwhelmed or getting confused by the process of ordering their medication when it was due. But if we knew that they had family or carers to help with the responsibilities, we would ask for their consent before taking them off the service.

Here's my attempt to explain what assembling a medication box entails: It can take anywhere from forty minutes (if they had only a few tablets) to two hours. It all depended on how many different tablets were required. I think we were sitting at roughly ninety patients who were on the weekly medication boxes.

A few patients agreed to revert back but most declined.

And somehow, by November 2020, we had more patients on medication boxes than ever.

And that wasn't all that I did on a day-to-day basis. I would also help in the dispensary which could quickly become very busy with patients waiting in the shop for their prescriptions. Sometimes, I would prepare methadone and often help out with the overwhelming backlog of prescriptions that get electronically sent to the pharmacy from various GP surgeries.

I was still doing the dispensing apprenticeship qualification when I could but finding time for it was challenging. A few times, I even worked on it at home without getting paid, just to attempt to finish it within the time frame.

Jake and I decided that work stress was no longer something I could tolerate. Our baby was our priority. We didn't want to put our pregnancy under unnecessary strain, especially after last time.

Jake earns a comfortable wage. He is a chicken farmer, and it's a family business; Jake, his brother, his dad, and his dad's cousin work there. They plan it so that they all have one day off each weekend (two of them work one day and the other two the next), but they all work during the week. It's hard graft for them, but they get back what they put in— a decent payday.

So, *luckily,* reducing my hours wasn't an issue.

My new working pattern was Monday, Tuesday and Wednesday, 9am to 1pm. I had a lunch break and worked from 2pm to 6pm. Then, on a Thursday, I would work from 9am to 1pm and have a long weekend. This meant that the boss had to bring in another pair of hands and they needed to be a trained dispenser, ready to fill my gaps. He arranged for someone from another pharmacy within the business to work the days I wasn't there. They would spread their working days between two different pharmacies every week.

...

I began to feel a lot less pressure from work and could focus on myself and growing our baby.

The private early scan date quickly approached. We arrived and were seen pretty much straight away.

The sonographer looked different this time. Maybe it was because I wasn't so emotionally drained that I could actually notice a person's appearance. She had ash blonde hair, wore glasses, was tall and spoke softly. I would say that she was around forty-five and she was still as lovely as I remembered her to be.

As she was preparing her equipment and entering my details, she told us her back story. She explained how she used to be a midwife in the NHS, then learnt sonography and opened up her own clinic a few years back. She is full of experience.

And, soon after, the time had come.

I lay on the bed, nervous but ready to see our baby. It was another internal scan due to being a young gestation.

It was still uncomfortable but it didn't feel as bad as it had done at our previous visit to her.

My eyes were eagerly scanning the screen. There was what looked like a little bean. That bean was our baby!

The sonographer pointed out where the heartbeat was faintly pumping away.

A heartbeat!

There was a heartbeat!

We were on cloud nine!

Due to the nature of our last visit to her, the sonographer also genuinely looked over the moon for us. Not that I don't believe she is with everyone that she sees but you could tell the relief and happiness she felt for us in that moment.

Thank you, God, Allah, Buddha, everyone!

I was six weeks and two days and feeling like shit. A promising sign; obviously!

But, oh my God; the nausea was relentless. It was like a seven-week hangover from six to thirteen weeks gestation. My morning sickness would occur at night, after my evening meal. I dreaded eating because I knew what I was to expect.

Christmas that year was full of joy and sickness. I suppose it was no different to every other Christmas. But this time, it wasn't the amount of food or prosecco causing me to hurl my guts up.

Work was also challenging when I felt sick all of the time, made worse by wearing a mask.

Five weeks after our early private scan, our hospital appointment for our NHS scan came through the post for the following week.

That first trimester had gone so fast, but the constant hang-over feeling was overwhelming and made it feel never-ending.

Everything at the twelve-week scan was fine. My little bean was growing nicely.

It was strange; the exact day that I transitioned into the second trimester, I didn't feel sick anymore. I am sorry to all the ladies who aren't so lucky with that.

I was still managing to run and do workouts. I had adapted them to be pregnancy-friendly, and an app gave me some new ideas for specific pregnancy workouts. You mimic the trainer's actions from the video, and the workouts are altered each trimester to accommodate the growing bump.

Being pregnant meant that the repeat smear test that would be due in February of 2021 would have to wait until around twelve weeks after the birth.

At nineteen weeks, we booked in to have a sex scan with the same private sonographer we had seen just thirteen weeks prior. Jake couldn't make that scan due to it being a busy period at the farm so my mum came with me. We didn't want to know at the scan anyway so it wasn't as if he was missing out on finding out the sex of his child. We asked the sonographer to write it down in an envelope so that we could find out at our gender reveal party we had planned for the upcoming Saturday.

The party was just going to be with our parents as it was still COVID-19 rules that no more than fifteen people (or something like that) could be together at one time. The rules changed so often that I couldn't keep up.

The little bean cooking in my stomach did not want to play ball. The sonographer couldn't determine the gender based on the position they were laid in and they refused to move regardless of whether I was lying on my side or on my back. She even sent me up and down the stairs in the building where her clinic was based. But my stubborn child wouldn't move; they were already taking after daddy.

After forty minutes of trying, she sent me off to McDonald's to have something sugary to eat in an attempt to wake the little bean up and move them. She told me to come back in forty minutes as she had another lady coming in for a scan after my original appointment.

The McDonald's we went to was only a two-minute drive from her clinic.

In my mum's car, we went to the drive-through and sat in the car park while I had a McFlurry and a full-fat Coke. Mum had the same as me. I mean, you can't go to McDonald's and watch someone else eat; it's nearly physically impossible!

And, of course, I had to use their facilities too; otherwise, my bladder would burst. Drinking a medium-sized McDonald's Coke just goes straight through a pregnant lady's renal system.

We drove back when it was time, and the little monkey was moving a lot. However, the sonographer was still struggling to get a clear picture of the gender. She stared at her screen for ages, scowling. This baby was testing our patience, a sign of what was to come. She had turned off the screen in our view so that we wouldn't accidentally notice something that would tell us their gender.

Eventually, she said, "I got a few flashes of the area I needed to examine but you have a naughty baby in there who was reluctant to reveal what they were. I'm 99% sure of what I saw."

She handed me two envelopes: one with *'DO NOT OPEN'* written on the front and the other with some scan photos that didn't reveal anything about the sex. I was dying to open the top-secret envelope.

She also informed me that I had placenta previa, a low-lying placenta that was slightly covering my internal cervix opening. She told me that sexual intercourse wasn't advised due to the risk of bleeding and placental abruption which is life-threatening for both mum and baby.

"Not a problem!" I said, maybe a bit too happily. But I wasn't feeling very sexy anyway, being pregnant.

When I got home, Jake was back from work and I broke the *dreadful* news of our sex ban.

"What, really?" he said.

Afraid so, babe.

The gender canisters I had ordered (one with blue confetti and one with pink) were also delivered while I was out. I immediately took them, along with the top secret envelope, to our next-door neighbours to look after until the party day.

They opened it and gave us back the cannon that matched the scan result. Or, so we hoped; they didn't seem the type to play a cruel trick on us like that!

Between the scan we had just had and the party day, we had our NHS twenty-week anomaly scan. Jake managed to come to this one. It was so hard not to ask what the gender was but temptation didn't get the better of either of us. *Willpower or what?*

Everything with the scan was fine but they didn't manage to get a measurement of the baby's spine so I had to go back in another two weeks. I asked about the placenta previa and it was still low-lying but it was only just covering my internal cervix opening.

Saturday, March 20th, 2021: gender reveal day! I was excited when I woke up that morning. I had been so patient all week that I had really shocked myself (and Jake).

I ordered a cake for the party from a local lady who bakes as a hobby. From what I had seen on social media, she has made all kinds of celebration cakes for people and I couldn't wait to try her cake; it looked amazing!

Jake's mum and I had driven down that morning to collect the cake. *Wow!* She had done a brilliant job! I know it probably seems OTT to have a cake for a party with only eight people present but it was a special day for us all.

We had the party at Jake's parent's house because that morning, Jake was helping take down a massive tree in the neighbour's garden at the back of ours that had hung over massively into our garden, and there were branches all over. The neighbour continued the noisy tree-chopping work without Jake that afternoon, as the supplies they had hired for the job needed to be returned not long after.

We picked up the top-secret envelope and the *hopefully* correct canister from the neighbour next door while walking up to Jake's parents' house. The canister had a tab on it, and underneath it was the colour of the confetti inside. Even when we were popping it, we couldn't see what colour it was going to be.

At 13:00, my mum, dad, stepdad, and dad's fiancé arrived. I was eager to get everyone a drink so that we could crack on and pop the cannon. However, impatience crept in thick and fast.

Everyone stood facing Jake and me. Jake was in charge of popping the canister, and we all counted down from five.

Four...

Three...

Two...

One...

BANG!

The confetti was blue.

WE WERE HAVING A BOY!

Either way, it would have been a complete shock but it also made the fact that we were having a baby a bit more real now that we could choose a name.

We told the rest of the family and everyone was buzzing. We were on a high and ready to start planning how to decorate our baby boys' room. Everything felt perfect.

Then, five days after the gender reveal, mine and my family's world was torn apart.

Chapter 8
The Day that Time Stood Still

"No one but ourselves can free our minds" - Bob Marley's redemption song (Marley, 1980)

Thursday March 25th 2021.

It was a typical Thursday morning for me; I worked at the pharmacy until 1pm. I was still behind on my deadlines for my apprenticeship so I spent the morning in the staff room, getting my head down to complete a backlog of work. I had to take a few standing breaks for comfort due to my growing belly but I hadn't done too badly. I managed to get through more than expected. However, I still had a way to go if I was going to complete my course before I went off on maternity leave; fifteen months after starting the apprenticeship.

I had planned to meet Jake at home after work and then go food shopping. Our house is just over a five-minute drive from the pharmacy, so I was home at around 13:10. He arrived back around 14:30, got changed, and then we headed to the same infamous Tesco store where we had bought all our pregnancy tests, one of those hadn't been on the shopping list for a while now.

Once we got home and finished unpacking the food shop, Jake began cooking tea while I put my feet up. Being pregnant does excuse you from a lot of jobs…

It was around 17:00. I was sitting on the sofa, about to drink a cup of tea, when my phone rang. I looked at the caller ID and it was my mum.

"Hi, Mum," I said. I could hear her trying to catch her breath, like she was having a panic attack.

"Jazz, are you at home?" she asked, almost like she was hyperventilating. "It's uncle Kev... he's took his own life." *What?*

I told my mum that I'd be straight round.

When I got off the phone, Jake looked at me like life had just drained from my body before him. I felt the colour fall from my face and my heart was beating so fast that, by this point, it felt like it was coming out of my chest.

"Uncle Kev has killed himself," I told him. And then I broke.

Jake was hugging me with tears in his eyes, trying to calm me down.

"I need to go to Mum. Stay here. I'll call you soon," I said.

Uncle Kev is my mum's older brother. Although there were thirteen years between them, he was my mum's rock, especially during the struggles of my grandparents getting older and becoming more dependent on them both for things such as life admin; bills and appointments, etc.

He was a man who everyone greatly loved. I know that sounds cliché when someone dies but he really was. He had so many friends; it was unreal! His humour was infectious and being around him was one of the best feelings in the world because his jovial personality inflicted happiness on people.

He was a family man; a husband with three children and five grandchildren. They were always doing things together and he loved spending time with his grandkids and his own children.

He had been married to my auntie long before I was born. They had two sons and a daughter, the youngest of the three.

My aunt is half-American and when I was around seven, they moved to California. Life seemed to be pretty good for them there. We visited when I was nine and I remember my mum being so excited to see her brother that she could burst.

We stayed with them at their home in Murrieta, about a ninety-minute car journey from Los Angeles. Our visit lasted two weeks and it was the best holiday ever. My uncle took us to Disneyland and SeaWorld and we visited Hollywood. It was incredible.

They moved back to the UK ten years later for visa reasons but I'm not overly sure of the details of why. They came back to Gainsborough town, where they lived before being uprooted to the States. It is about a forty-minute drive from Lincoln where my nan, grandad and mum lived; it was the place that he grew up in.

He worked in auto-electrics for most of his life and his last job was tutoring the subject at the local college. He was a massive supporter of his Gainsborough Trinity

Football Club; he even had his own bench outside their football ground.

Everyone knew him. Even in the pub that I worked at from the age of seventeen to twenty, there would be punters who came in who knew him and had stories to tell of his humorous ways. He was a legend. And still is.

I made the one-minute walk to Mum's house. Well, it's not really a minute; it's slightly over seventy seconds (I've timed it).

When I walked in my mum's front door, she was pacing her living room, looking at her phone.

"I can't get hold of your sister!" she said, flustered and shaking.

She was alone; my stepdad was at the funeral home, seeing his dad at rest before the funeral the following day. *Talk about timing.*

"Put the phone down, Mum," I said through blurry, tear-filled eyes. I encouraged her hand, which she had her phone in, down to her side and I brought her into me with my arms wrapped around her as she broke again. We both did.

After several minutes of holding her, I said, "Mum, tell me what happened." I encouraged her to lift her face off my shoulder. She managed to explain what she knew while her breath was still jumping; it was as if she couldn't get enough air into her lungs.

My cousin phoned her around thirty minutes before we were having this conversation. This meant that, half an hour ago, a piece of my mum's heart left that would never return.

He told her that Kev's wife (my auntie Yvette) found him in their garage around 14:00 that day. He had hung himself. That was all she knew at that moment in time.

I felt sick.

We both broke down again and my stepdad arrived back simultaneously, along with his sister.

Mum had managed to speak to him on the phone before ringing me. He had picked up a missed call from her when leaving the funeral home and immediately phoned her back.

"Do nan and grandad know?" I asked Mum.

"No," she sobbed. "I need to tell them but I don't know how."

Jake arrived very soon after, without me even calling him— *caring and supportive, Jake.*

He came in, and when he saw my mum, he put his arms around her while she sobbed into his arms. This made me break even more. My stepdad's sister had a hold of me and was trying her best to calm me down from my emotional outburst; it was for my own benefit as well as that of the baby inside me.

Oh yeah, I had forgotten about him for the last hour.

My stepdad must have felt so overwhelmed but also robbed of his grief. He was about to bury his dad, who was the last of his parents he was saying goodbye to. But he now had to be strong for my mum and our family so we could try and get through each step of this shocking and unthinkable situation.

When you get told the news of someone's death, especially that of a family member or close friend, it can be hard to digest or to really believe it. Maybe it's harder to come to terms with because of the circumstances around how the person has died. For example, if someone had a terminal illness, is that any easier to get the inevitable news compared to hearing that someone has decided they don't want to live anymore?

All I knew was that what I felt about the death of my uncle was the tip of the iceberg compared to how much my auntie, cousins, grandparents and mum must have been hurting.

I can't pretend that I understand what drives someone to take their own life, and I'm not sure I would ever want to. But it's hard not to over think why people do it without knowing what pushed them to that point. It can send you crazy.

Sadly, my uncle left no note explaining why he took this course of action. But would that make it easier? I hate to dwell on what could have happened but I think that an explanation might have helped everyone understand why he chose to leave. Maybe even provided a minuscule amount of closure? I don't know.

Death is brutal and complex to come to terms with, no matter how the person dies. In my opinion, what makes suicide more challenging to get over is the shock value that comes along with it; the choice a person has to live or die.

But what an intentional death leaves behind has similar consequences to any other, whether it is natural or accidental. The heartache, the questions, the grief, the anger and the loneliness their families feel are always the same. However, when it comes to suicide (especially ones without an explanation), these emotions attack with next-level venom that plays cruel tricks on the mind.

When my mum told me about Uncle Kev, it felt as if time stood still. But it doesn't, does it?

Time is relentless. We live in a world where everything about our reality is determined by time. We count the time down until a special event. Time is what decides how long we are on this earth, how long we have good health and how long we get to spend with loved ones. Time can be on your side; it can be the best healer or the worst villain. It gives with one hand but takes away with another.

Time, you are a narcissistic, controlling prick.

The only thing I can tell you is (what *I think I* know), that how my uncle chose to take his life is a very definite way of doing it. It's not like overdosing on tablets with the chance of being found and revived. No. This is final, and all I can do is respect his choice.

A few hours later, my sister arrived. You could tell that she had been crying but she looked like she had got it together when I saw her. She had just driven an hour from where she lived so she needed some sort of composure to make the journey.

My sister went with my mum and stepdad to my grandparents' house while Jake and I brought Mum's little dog back to our house; she didn't know how long that visit was going to last.

My grandad had recently been diagnosed with dementia. Still, it was clear his brain impairment had started quite a while before his diagnosis.

He was such a funny man. He had humour just like my uncle; his son. When we had family get-togethers, it would be like a comedy show and everyone in the room would be crying with laughter. I miss those times.

Even with his diagnosis, his humour still shone through; the dementia wasn't taking that away from him first.

He used to demand that he always had the most up-to-date gadgets, but he had no idea how to use them. My mum and Kev would take the brunt of him; they even showed him how to get the football scores up on his smartphone. It was like the world had ended when he couldn't see the *Sky Sports Score* app. It was pretty comical at times, I can't lie.

But then, the news of the death of his son began to deteriorate his dementia rapidly. And he, the funny, doting husband, father and grandad we once knew, was rapidly being taken from us.

We called my nan 'Little Nana' because she was so small. Although she shrank with age, she was never really tall. She was a frail lady but also the strongest woman I've ever known, just like my mum. She was my angel and still is.

My poor nana's heart was already breaking. She was beginning to lose the husband she had known for over sixty years of marriage to a cruel disease. And then, to learn the news that her son willingly took his own life must have shattered her. In fact, I know it did. How does a mother comprehend losing her child at any age? It's not how the circle of life is supposed to work. That makes me angry.

I don't know much about the reactions of either grandparent being told about the death of their son. Still, forever after, my sweet soul, Little Nana, would spend the rest of her days silently heartbroken.

The following day, it was my stepdad's father's funeral. It was a day of heightened emotions already, let alone when you add learning the news of my uncle not twenty-four hours prior. It was tough for everyone but my mum must have been going through hell. To hold her husband's hand while he lays his dad to rest, and also just beginning the whirlwind emotions of grief for her brother, is an unthinkable situation to be put in.

It's the funny thing about the world we live in and how quickly our lives can change. In just a second, we can go from being on cloud nine to plummeting into rock bottom.

Time again; showing its true colours.

I didn't go back to work the following week. My mum and I spent every day at my grandparents' house, supporting them. My mum had a lot of admin to do as both she and her brother had power of attorney for my grandparents. Death is another way for the admin to show its ugly, tedious face.

It was emotionally draining but there was nowhere else I wanted to be. But very little was spoken about my uncle. My grandparents hardly brought him up, and my grandad would sometimes get frustrated and angry if someone did.

Nana had a carer in the morning and evening to help her with personal hygiene and getting dressed. She thought so highly of them, and they were a good support for her, physically and emotionally, but also a welcomed distraction.

Although I was mentally elsewhere, I went back to work the following week, two weeks before the funeral. I needed the money because I wasn't getting paid for being off. It wasn't classed as compassionate leave because he was my uncle and that apparently isn't a close enough relative to require compassion about, let alone the circumstances under which he died.

I can't remember exactly how long after my uncle died but my mum, nan, stepdad and I went to visit him at the chapel of rest. I think maybe two weeks. My grandad wasn't feeling great and wanted to visit another time.

It was the first time that I'd seen a dead body. It was so strange; he sort of resembled a wax figure.

I stood there staring at him. A small part of me felt on edge, like he was going to open his eyes and shout *boo!* He didn't, obviously.

It was heartbreaking, though. Seeing my mum lean over his coffin, telling him how much she loves him and will miss him, was the most painful thing I've ever witnessed.

My nan sat in a chair near the coffin while my stepdad and I said our goodbyes. We then waited outside so she could talk to her son for the last time. My mum stayed with her.

...

Monday April 19th, 2021.

The day had come to say goodbye.

I drove my grandparents, mum, and stepdad to my uncle's home. All the close family was there waiting for the hearse and funeral cars to arrive. It was a tense morning. People were chatting amongst themselves about day-to-day life and catching up, while others were silent, and some were crying. It was the strangest scenario I've ever encountered. I didn't know where to put myself. I don't think anybody did.

The hearse arrived, and I felt the hairs on my neck begin to stand.

We got into the cars and followed the hearse to *Gainsborough Crematorium*.

On the way, we drove past my uncle's beloved football team's stadium, and there must have been at least two hundred people standing on the path outside, clapping as the hearse went by.

Amongst the crowd, at the end of the line, there were mechanics in various coloured overalls from different garages in Gainsborough. I remember seeing red, navy and green colours in them but I'm sure there was more. What a sign of respect.

Various people were also dotted all along the route from my uncle's house to just outside the crematorium. The amount of love shown to him was so emotionally overwhelming. And, just imagine if the COVID-19 measures weren't restricting funerals to just fifteen people. In that case, I guarantee every single one of those people would have been at the service, too.

To this day, we still don't know why he committed suicide and I know it tortures my family every day. His wife, his children and his sister (my mum) are remarkable for how they keep on going, even when the torture feels like it's becoming too much to withstand. When anger throws rationality out the window because of all the unanswered questions, closure seems like it will never happen. They have had to learn a new way of living with grief and without this part of them that is missing.

We all have.

Chapter 9
A New Chapter

After my uncle's funeral, it was tough for everyone. The emotional rollercoaster was so hard to navigate. At the time, I was twenty-five weeks pregnant and I was feeling the pressure of time running away from me. *Time, again, being a twat.*

Due to being off work quite a bit in the last month, I was behind on my apprenticeship deadline. I had a lot of work to do which was causing me so much anxiety; I just needed to get it done.

When I returned to work a week after the funeral, I spoke to my area manager and told him that I needed time to get this done. Due to the lack of staff, it was becoming an impossible task.

As COVID-19 had caused a lot of vulnerable people to shield, our regular pharmacist (our manager) was not at work due to her pregnancy; she had fallen pregnant just as the pandemic hit and was immediately relieved of duty.

However, the rules had changed for pregnant women by the time I fell in November 2020 and we no longer needed to shield.

Completing my apprenticeship was challenging as we had different pharmacists every day who needed the support of the dispensary team for minor things such as where we kept stuff, patient information, etc.; things a regular pharmacist would know. The boss used locum dispensers to help in the dispensary, while I spent a good chunk of time in the staff room attending to my course.

By the time I was twenty-eight weeks pregnant, I had flown through the never-ending burden of my apprenticeship. The last thing to do was to have an examiner come in and assess me on my knowledge and watch me work.

I also had to do a paper exam. It was so intense. It was a daunting day. I felt so on edge and I remember my baby boy cooking away in my belly, kicking me in my ribs as I was trying to concentrate! *Thanks for that, you little monkey.*

I didn't care what result I got in the end; I just wanted it over with.

A couple of weeks later, my results came back in the post. I told my colleague to open it because I didn't have any faith and couldn't bring myself to look.

She opened it and said, "Jazz, come here."

I went and she handed me the paper, saying: "You are going to want to look."

My overall grade for my coursework and exam was a distinction.

A distinction.... How?!

I was over the moon.

But I don't know how I had managed to complete the course in time before I left for maternity leave, let alone get a distinction. I balanced it with pandemic stresses, a miscarriage, a pregnancy and losing my uncle. It was a lot...

That gave me confidence in myself; confidence that I can work under pressure, confidence that I can do academics, confidence in my resilience and confidence that I can do more.

During my third trimester, I felt like a slight weight had been lifted off my shoulders by completing my apprenticeship. However, the grief was still hitting my family hard which is not unsurprising in the slightest.

My mum and I were still spending quite a bit of time at my grandparents' house. My grandad's dementia was getting progressively worse. I won't talk about the things he began to do because I have too much respect for him. But, let's put it this way: my nan had a lot to deal with, and it was heartbreaking to see her lose the person that she loved— another emotional rollercoaster.

I began my maternity leave when I was thirty-six weeks gestation. At this point, I was still working out at the gym which had reopened after closing due to the pandemic.

By then, my workouts consisted of a few bodyweight squats, bicep curls, and resistance training for my lower body. I was frightened of tearing in labour, so I kept my lower body as strong as possible.

I had my midwife's appointment at 38+1 weeks gestation and she measured my pregnant belly (as they did at every appointment from around twenty-four weeks). But this was a different midwife than the usual lady I would see at my antenatal appointments.

When she compared her measurement to the previous measurement, she showed no growth in the last two weeks. She repeated it several times to ensure a consistent answer and it was the same so she referred me for a growth scan at the hospital. She explained that the measurement may be off because she was a different midwife, but it was best to get checked with a growth scan. I was slightly apprehensive after that.

Another fucking thing going wrong.

Great!

But I kept calm.

I had my appointment on Friday morning that week and I was 38+4 weeks gestation.

There was a girl in the waiting area that I sort of knew from when we were teenagers. I didn't know her all that well but we had crossed paths a few times. We sat chatting and she was also there for a growth scan. She was in front of me by two days in her pregnancy and she was having her second baby.

Soon, I was taken in; they scanned me and his estimated weight was 6 lbs 7 oz.

Following the scan, I had a chat with the doctor who offered me an induction of labour because, although he was an okay size and everything else was normal, they felt that it was best.

Being a first-time mum without much knowledge of induction or childbirth, I followed the advice of the professionals. They booked me for an induction the next day.

I called Jake as soon as I left and told him we needed to get stuff sorted. He left the farm pretty much straight after that phone call and was home by 14:00.

When I got home, I began cleaning; it was a session like no other. When Jake arrived, he also mucked in, and we blitzed the house. *Nesting, I suppose.*

I re-packed my *already*-packed hospital bag to make sure that we had everything that we needed.

Then we went food shopping as we had nothing in and no one wants to come home to a food-less house.

We were rushing around like a pair of Duracell bunnies on caffeine. Well, as fast as a heavily pregnant woman can rush.

The girl I had been chatting to in the waiting room at the scan appointment messaged me on Facebook Messenger and told me that she was admitted that day for induction. I would hopefully see her the following day when I arrived at the hospital.

That evening, we went up to Jake's parent's house for tea. It is literally 'up' as we have to go up a slight hill to get there.

At about 17:00 on the walk there, I was stopped in my tracks by a tightening pain. I had been having them for weeks, but they were 'Braxton Hicks', and this felt different. It wasn't overly painful and they were on and off all evening.

We stopped off at my mum's on the way home as we walked past her house to get to Jake's parents. She was getting very excited and was timing how frequently they were coming. I can't remember precisely how frequent they were but it wasn't anything significant.

When I got into bed that night, the tightenings had completely stopped.

I sort of half expected to be woken up by my waters going and then go into full-blown labour, like they do on telly, but that didn't happen.

The next morning, Jake went to work and I got ready to go to the hospital. My mum picked me up at 08:50 and drove me to the maternity wing.

I was booked in to go to the antenatal/postnatal ward at 09:00 and it's only a five-minute drive from my house. *Very handy!*

I was admitted to the ward and shown to my bed space. It was a bay full of pregnant women; they try to keep the antenatal and postnatal women separate.

The girl I had seen the previous day at the scan messaged me, and she came into my bay for a chat. All the women there, including me, were sitting on the pregnancy balls, chatting away. We were having a good old laugh, and one of the midwives came in and said, "It sounds like you lot are having a great time!" *like we were naughty kids.*

Birthing partners were allowed to visit from 14:00 at that time for COVID-19 reasons, so we all went our separate ways when they arrived. Jake was there to hold my hand through the induction process, which was quite uncomfortable. But the midwife told me that I was already

2cm dilated, so the tightening at home must have been doing something.

They used the hormone pessary to try and get my labour progressing and then it was just a waiting game.

I began having some tightenings again, but they were still irregular.

That night, one of the women in my bay was sent up to the labour ward at about 03:30 in the morning and I didn't manage to get back to sleep after that. I was uncomfortable and I could hear other patients and the midwives outside our bay. I gave up trying about two hours later, put my headphones on and watched *Love Island* on my iPad.

On Sunday, my pessary had fallen out in the toilet that afternoon. I wasn't due my review to see if the pessary had made any changes to my cervix for a good six hours. But the doctor decided to check me and told me that they would be able to break my waters.

The irregular tightenings came and went the next day while I waited for the labour ward to have me available. Jake was getting impatient but I was surprisingly calm and didn't feel the need to rush; for once.

I was so tired by Tuesday morning when the labour ward midwives came and got me; I had woken up at 03:30 that morning and the one before also. But adrenaline made it difficult to sleep.

I rang Jake and told him that I was being transferred and he was buzzing; he came straight to the maternity wing and headed to the labour ward.

My midwives looking after me were amazing. I had a very experienced one who told me that she was a labour ward coordinator. I also had an excellent first-year midwifery student. They were so supportive of both me and Jake.

At 10:00, the doctor broke my waters and advised me to go on the hormone drip straight away to help induce contractions and make my cervix dilate.

The baby's heartbeat was constantly recorded to determine how they were coping with the synthetic hormone and the machine also recorded my contractions. I was attached to a drip with antibiotics flowing through every four hours as, at 16 weeks gestation, I had been detected to have Group B Strep; a bacteria that can be harmful to the baby when being birthed vaginally. Antibiotics are given in labour prophylactically for it.

The hormone drip was a bitch. *Next level bitch.* The pain I had been feeling prior was ramped up a thousand times more. Four hours later, I requested the epidural, and once that kicked in, labour became a pleasant experience.

I managed to sleep! Finally! Some sleep that was undisrupted by surrounding noise or from being uncomfortable. I had the best two-hour nap that I was going to get for a long time!

At 16:30, the midwife checked my labour progression. I was then 8cm dilated and nearly effaced (my cervix had shortened in length), which was brilliant progress for a primigravida woman (meaning anyone who was going through childbirth for the first time).

At about 17:30, the doctors came to do their ward rounds. They came into my room, checked in with how I was feeling and advised me on their ideal plan. They told me that the midwife was going to recheck me in an hour as they could see from the machine recording that the contractions were coming very regularly. They could tell from the baby's heartbeat trace that he was coping fine. Apparently, I had made good progress from my waters being broken and the hormone drip starting.

When it comes to physically checking a woman's progression of labour, it is done through vaginal examination. Ideally, it shouldn't be carried out an awful lot due to the risk of infection. Still, as I was already on antibiotics for bacterial infection, it was probably a risk that they weren't as worried about.

However, the midwife didn't want to do another vaginal examination that soon after and didn't feel it was necessary.

One hour passed, and I began to feel some pressure, more than I had been doing. Even though I had the epidural, I could still feel pressure but without the pain.

The midwife examined me and told me that I was fully dilated. She advised me to have a passive hour to let the baby come down a bit further on his own so that I didn't have to work so hard.

An hour passed.

It was near the end of their shift, and I was hoping the student would be able to deliver my baby as it would count towards the forty births that she needed to qualify.

The midwife told me to start pushing when I was ready, in line with the contractions that I could still feel were happening; they just didn't hurt. That was until I got the go-ahead to push, and then I suddenly couldn't feel them anymore. The midwife put her hand on my belly and directed me to push when a contraction was present.

After around twenty minutes of pushing, our beautiful baby boy was born. He was perfect. I felt a huge rush of love. I felt *fortunate.*

Frankie John Fields was born at 19:53. He weighed 7 lbs and 6 oz, the opposite of what was estimated at the scan!

And I didn't tear! *Thank you, squats and resistant bands.*

Jake and I were on cloud nine. However, about three hours after I gave birth to Frankie, Jake began violently being sick in the delivery room bathroom.

He had caught the sickness bug my mum and stepdad had come down with the day before, which meant that he had to leave straight away.

Frankie and I were moved down to the postnatal ward at about 02:00 on the Wednesday morning. I think I managed about two hours of sleep in total around Frankie and the other babies on the ward crying, letting everyone know they wanted their food or their nappies changing.

Later that day, I wasn't allowed any other visitors other than my birth partner, as it was during COVID-19 restrictions. And he obviously couldn't come, anyway. I felt a bit sad when the other women had their partners with them, enjoying their baby bubble while I was just sitting with Frankie, wishing that Jake was with me.

I texted his mum, asking if she could pick me up when I was ready to be discharged later that day; I wanted Frankie and me to go to her house because Jake was at home poorly. That was the plan until Jake's brother, who lived with his parents, told his mum that he wasn't feeling very well (with symptoms linked to COVID-19).

He took a lateral flow test, and it came back positive.

Shit! Now what?

So, the plan changed to Jake moving into my mum's house where the sick people were. Jake's mum and sister came to my house before I got home, wearing full PPE, disinfecting everywhere and changing the bed sheets.

My sister drove from her home in Sheffield to pick me up and bring Frankie and me home from the hospital. *What a nightmare!*

When I got home, my sister said that she would stay overnight to help me. Jake's sister, who didn't live at home, also came for the whole evening.

My mum, Jake and stepdad came to the living room window to see us. When I held Frankie up so that his daddy could see him, it hit me like a tonne of bricks. I so desperately wanted him here with me. This was not the way that it was supposed to happen!

After they left, my sister and Jake's sister told me to go to bed. By this point, I was exhausted. I only managed about an hour before my phone made a notification noise and disturbed me. But I was quickly on high alert again for my baby.

I went downstairs and got some food. Then, I got myself properly ready for bed and took Frankie up with me this time.

I was so on edge all night. With every bit of noise that he made, I would roll over and stick my head into his Moses basket to check if he was okay and that he was breathing. That he wasn't cold. That he wasn't hot. That he wasn't dribbling sick. *Paranoid first-time mum.* I think that I got about four hours in total of sleep that night.

The following day, my mum told me that she hadn't been sick for forty-eight hours, so she was clear to come over. I was so happy when she did. Not that my sister wasn't helping, but I felt like I just needed my mum if I couldn't have Jake.

Jake came and stood in the front garden later that day to see us. We ended up going for a distant walk around the village with Frankie in his pram. We walked to his mum's and stood on their driveway so that they could also meet their grandson at a distance.

It was nice but also heartbreaking at the same time.

Again, that night, I had very little sleep. It was like I didn't want to sleep because Jake wasn't there next to me, listening out for him either. Every noise woke me. My mum slept in the other room and she woke to make him a bottle when he was crying for a feed while I changed him.

The next morning, I began vacuuming. Mum had told me not to, but I felt absolutely fine, and it wasn't a battle that she was winning. I like a clean house; it makes me feel better.

I cleaned while she fed and cuddled Frankie.

Jake was also due to come out of his isolation that day. He had been sick-free for forty-eight hours in the afternoon, and I wanted a nice, clean house for when he got home. But it turned out we needed him home a lot sooner than that!

Mum and I were sitting in the living room. I had just finished cleaning, and Frankie was asleep in his Moses basket when my mum saw something out of the corner of her eye.

"Oh my god," she'd said, wide-eyed like she had just seen a ghost.

"What? What is it?" I said with caution.

She thought that she had just seen a rat come past the living room door!

Great! That's just fucking great. With a newborn baby in the house, we also have a rat!

I got up and peeked around the door to see if I could spot it. It wasn't there. I checked the stairs, and it wasn't there either; it couldn't have travelled up the stairs in that time. It also wasn't in the bathroom downstairs, so it must have been in the kitchen.

I went and shut the kitchen door, ringing Jake in panic mode.

"You have to come home now. I mean *now*! There is a rat in our kitchen!"

Several seconds later, there was scratching at the kitchen door, and it wasn't the cat. She was upstairs asleep on my bed.

OH MY GOD!

Moments later, Jake came running around the corner from my mum's house and burst into the house like the number one rat-catcher. He kicked the kitchen door so that it would push the rat away as he went in. *It was so dramatic.* And Jake, being Jake, saved the day!

He said that it was just a mouse that Pumba (our cat) had brought in! *Naughty cat!*

Once the mouse ordeal was over and Mum had left to go home, I welcomed Jake home with open arms, full of relief that he was finally where he belonged: with us, ready to begin our new chapter of parenthood.

Chapter 10
Postnatal Depression Label Not Required

Disclaimer: This chapter talks about my early days in my postnatal journey and mental health. People's circumstances and other aspects of life are different, and it isn't like this for everyone. It's a complex topic as it is. It's not that I didn't love my baby or didn't feel blessed that he was healthy and in my arms because I one-thousand percent did. I just struggled, like so many women do, and that needs normalising.

When I was in the hospital having Frankie, I told Jake that I wanted to pursue midwifery further down the line. Doing as well as I had in my pharmacy apprenticeship, especially under all the circumstances I had faced while undertaking the course, made me feel that I could strive for more. I was even surer following the birth of my son because the experience of childbirth made me move past my intolerance for female reproductive parts, the same ones that I could barely stand to hear the words of when I was younger.

With that, I felt like I could pursue what was once a path in life I wanted to take—or at least give it a shot.

My conversation with Jake about wanting to do it was not in-depth; it was more like a passing comment. He said that it would be okay to do it in five years or so, but that was just an off-the-cuff idea of a timeline. And no more was said.

However, it turned out to happen sooner.

The postnatal period should be the happiest time of your life, right?

Don't get me wrong, I was over the moon to have a healthy baby who I adored so much but fuck, I found it challenging.

Day four, when my milk came in, was brutal. It was Jake's first full day back with us after his isolation at my mum's house. I was so emotional, tired and in pain with my chest. I couldn't breastfeed due to my breast reduction, and a slight bit of guilt crept in. Not that I should have felt that way because, if I hadn't had the operation, I probably wouldn't have had Frankie. The mind plays horrible tricks on you at times.

I also began to feel guilty about the miscarriage that I'd had only two weeks before falling pregnant with Frankie. Guilty that I didn't grieve *enough* or that I moved on too quickly.

In the first few weeks of Frankie's life, after Jake returned to work following paternity leave, I found it hard to adjust to the new way of life that I thought I was prepared for. It was hard to adapt to broken sleep. It was hard not to feel isolated when going from a social job and seeing people daily to sitting in the house with no adult interaction. But I wasn't ready to leave the house on my own with my newborn; I was almost scared.

It was hard to realise that I couldn't just go for a run or to the gym, two things that positively impacted my mental health. I couldn't just nip to the shop without it feeling like an overwhelming military operation. Constantly thinking about what you need when you go anywhere with a baby is draining. The checklists you do in your head can fill you with anxiety that makes your head want to burst. And, nine times out of ten, you have forgotten something; it either ruins your whole day and puts you in a shit mood, or you feel like a terrible mother.

Adjusting to motherhood means adapting to a new way of managing the passing of time. From timed feeds to nappy changes, medicine if needed, laundry, household duties, and not forgetting to eat, it all seems hazy, time again being a controlling prick. Well, that's how it felt for me.

When your partner comes home from work, he asks you how your day has been and what you have done, but you are sometimes unsure how to answer because it has been a blur. You're just relieved to be able to talk to someone who's not a baby and can provide a response. All you have done all day is try to keep yourself entertained while running on a lack of sleep and trying to cope with the whirlwind that is happening inside your body. Plus, being on constant alert for the next demand from your baby is tough.

Due to the lack of sleep, postnatal hormone crash and family circumstances, I began to struggle without realising it.

I started to feel envious of Jake going to work and getting a break. Because, at work, you get a break. You can have a tea break and drink it while it's hot. You can have a toilet break where you aren't needed because the baby is crying, sick or has a *poonami* covering their freshly-cleaned clothes or sheets of their Moses basket.

Every day felt like *Groundhog Day*. I needed something else. I could feel my mind beginning to seek stimulation. I thought that I needed more than what I was supposed to be enjoying at that moment, and my brain was telling me to do more while being a new mum just at home. It was like time was against me.

So, I started looking into midwifery.

When Frankie was five weeks old, my mum went on a much-needed holiday after the last five months of hell for her because of her brother and everything else with my grandparents. Obviously, she was so happy to have Frankie, but she needed to get away. I didn't blame her at all. She needed it for her own mental well-being.

However, that meant I was the first port of call for my grandparents as I lived ten minutes away. I had several phone calls from my nan that required me to go around to their house, which wasn't easy with my newborn. It was mainly for help with grandad or for collecting medication that they needed and taking it to them.

Once, my nan's carer called me because my grandad had a fall; I needed to go to their house and wait with them for the ambulance. Luckily, it was towards the end of the day, and Jake's mum was back from work, so she could have Frankie until either myself or Jake was back.

The carer also phoned my Auntie Yvette. She arrived about forty minutes after me and told me to go home, even though she was having a bad day emotionally. She said that I looked like I needed to rest. I felt like it, too. I must have looked tired.

A few days later, I attended my six-week postnatal check-up at the doctor's. I was in a state. I told her everything that had happened/happening in our family, as well as about the feelings that I was experiencing. She was lovely. Postnatal depression has crossed my mind briefly, and I asked her if that's what I was going through.

She'd said, "It sounds like you have been through a huge trauma that is still unfolding itself. I think you need time. We don't need to label anything. If you feel you are struggling or things get worse in a few weeks, we can prescribe some medication to try and help."

The thought of medication scared me. The stigma frightened me. The adjustment period of starting a new medication filled me with dread. I had this idea of never being able to come off them if I started.

Instead, she prescribed me the contraceptive pill that I was taking before pregnancy. However, it eventually made me decline further.

When Frankie was seven weeks old, I started an access to higher education course at my local college. Not everyone agreed with my choice, but my mum and best friend actively spurred me on. Even though now, I would say they thought that I wouldn't be able to manage it, they never told me that I couldn't. They just showed encouragement at the time because, at that moment, that's what I needed.

Telling someone, especially someone like me, that they can't or shouldn't do something only pushes them further into doing it, even more so when their brain isn't in a rational state.

Jake was frustrated and confused. He couldn't understand why having our baby wasn't enough for me. However, he still supported me at that time, no matter how much it hurt him. I found it hard to articulate how and what I was feeling because I wasn't really sure. I felt like I didn't want to waste time doing nothing while my baby slept. I felt useless.

It never crossed my mind about what it would be like further down the line when Frankie wouldn't sleep so much. I didn't know what the pattern of a child was like because I had never had one. But, at that moment, all he did was sleep, eat and poop and, with me not thinking rationally, I didn't see beyond this. Some may read this and wonder how I possibly thought that's all he would ever do, but I didn't.

My only thought was that I could do everything around feeds and naps; I couldn't see the problem.

This sparked the conversation about having more children as Jake told me that he wanted them to be close in age. However, this was something that we had never spoken about until I was looking into midwifery. He didn't mean immediately but was talking about wanting more in a year or two. But the thought of having another one scared me. And, even though my mind wasn't working as it should, I knew that I wanted to be a midwife. That was a conversation that didn't get resolved for a while.

In mid-September, I was due to go out with my friend from work for bottomless brunch for her big birthday celebrations. I was so excited. However, the timing clashed with a party that Jake's parents were having that evening; his mum was on Frankie duty, so she didn't drink.

It was the first time that I had gone out after having Frankie. The first time, I was drinking alcohol after everything that had happened that year. And I did not end up in a good way.

I enjoyed the bottomless brunch but I got far too drunk.

I went back to Jake's parent's house with the idea of joining the party but I wasn't thinking straight. I wish I had just gone home. I just wanted to shut myself away from the world; and so I did. I spent three hours until it was time to go home, talking to Jake's auntie in one of the bedrooms. I must have been saying so much rubbish that didn't make sense but I can only remember wanting to escape the reality that I was living.

I felt so emotional, guilty, angry and grief-stricken. I hadn't mourned for the baby that we lost or for my uncle. And also, the situation with my grandparents was breaking my heart. I was still obviously worried about my mum as well and how she was coping with everything. The last thing she needed was to worry about me but, thankfully, she wasn't at the party.

I knew that Jake and his mum were upset with me. Jake was upset because I didn't want to come out and see him, and his mum was upset because of that and since I hadn't gone near Frankie. But I remember not wanting to. I didn't want to be near my baby in the state that I was in.

Days after, I hated myself. I *loathed* myself. I thought about ringing the doctors and asking for the pills to help me, but I remembered everything that I was scared about when it came to taking them. So, I didn't. I should have.

I tried to explain myself to Jake's mum the following week, but I didn't manage to. I went to her house when I knew there wasn't anyone else there, and we sat down to talk about it. She told me how much it hurt her to see Jake like that, and before I could explain myself, I suddenly lost the courage to talk. I just cried and apologised.

Jake's mum and I can talk about anything because I see her like a second mum. She's also a friend. But that's the only thing I have never been able to say.

Writing is so much easier to put your words into words.

But, at the end of the day, she is his mother; that's her baby, and I was the one to upset him. She wasn't shouting at me or talking in a way that made me think that I was a horrible person. She was just expressing her concern for her child, like any mother would. And I respect that.

A few weeks later, my baby was rapidly changing. He was sleeping less and needing my attention more. I gave up the ghost with the access course; I couldn't focus on the amount required to get the grades that I would need to apply to university. I felt like I had failed myself, but I hadn't.

As the days went by, things were becoming easier with having a baby. *I can do this*, I remember thinking.

The thought of going out on my own with him was becoming less daunting. I began to feel confident going to the local children's centre a few days a week and attending baby groups.

I remember plucking up the courage to take him out alone for the first time. We only went to ASDA Living, but I felt like it was an accomplishment. He even vomited all over me, himself and the cafe floor. Still, I tackled that one step at a time. Slowly but surely, I began to find my feet while still learning this new way of living: motherhood.

I had my long overdue smear test in October 2021. The result came back positive with HPV again. *Fucking great.* That really helped my fragile mind. *Not.*

The letter told me that I would require another smear test again in a year to check if it had turned itself into cancer. It was always playing on my mind.

Chapter 11
Whirlwind Emotions

My uncle's death played a part in the poor postnatal mental health that I experienced in the first few months of Frankie's life. How could it not? When I managed to sleep, I would often dream about him and how he died, maybe because I had time to think while at home with no other distractions.

Because of my lack of sleep, I once thought that I saw him in my living room doorway in the middle of the night while I was feeding Frankie. But again, my mind was playing tricks on me.

I believe in spirits, but I have never seen one. I've felt things that make me think I might not be alone when no one else is in the house, such as noises like cupboard doors opening and shutting, but I never physically saw them. I just heard them.

On a few occasions, at times which were coincidental regarding the topic of conversation, Frankie's toys switched themselves on, and Jake was also there to witness them. So, who knows? Maybe I am, or maybe I'm not crazy.

The rapid deterioration of my grandad was hard to go through. The heartbreak that my nan was witnessing day in and day out began to take its toll on us all.

In November 2021, it eventually became unsafe for my grandparents to have grandad living at home. He needed 24/7 care. That was hard for my mum; she needed her brother's support, and I could feel her frustration with him during that transition.

Although my nan knew it was in her and grandad's best interest, she wanted her husband back home with her.

Nan's cleaner, who she had come round once a week, had just retired, so while on maternity leave, I began to clean on a day when Mum had an extended lunch break to look after Frankie.

While cleaning another room, I used to see my Nan in her living room. My heart hurt for her. She would just sit there, either reading or in silence. It was like she was slowly fading away. She didn't have the television on much during the day, either; she just liked the peace.

Between my mum, my Auntie Yvette, and myself, we took my nana to the nursing home where my grandad was living on the other side of the city. It wasn't always a pleasant visit. Sometimes, he would be angry and often confused when we were there.

He was also diagnosed with bowel cancer not long after moving into the nursing home and refused any treatment. I don't blame him.

In December 2021, Frankie was nearly five months old, and I began to look for jobs to go back to that would work around having a baby and provide better money. I applied for a few jobs within the NHS, some bank work and some flexible working.

I knew that I wouldn't be far off wanting to go back to work. It sounds mad, I know. I already had the best job in the world, being a mum. Still, in my head, I needed to go back to have a sense of purpose again because the job that I had done before was constantly full-on, and I missed my normality.

Just after the New Year, I interviewed for a job as a therapy rehabilitation assistant for NHS Community Health Services. I was offered the position just a few days later, and they quickly began the enrolment process of requesting a DBS check and the relevant paperwork needed to be employed by the NHS.

That Christmas was a whirlwind of emotions. It was the first Christmas for the family without my Uncle Kev and the first Christmas with Frankie.

My Auntie Yvette and cousin went to California to visit my other cousin who lives there that Christmas.

My mum brought my grandad and nan to her house for the day. It was lovely to see them together again, not in a communal area of a nursing home or grandad's bedroom. He was where he belonged on Christmas, with his family.

But that Christmas, I was in a state of emotion that I found hard to control, and I had a few outbursts of excessive crying.

I knew it was probably the last Christmas my family would have with my grandad, and all I could think about was how quickly everything was changing and how our lives had been turned upside down in the last year. It was hard for any of us to keep up.

In the New Year, grandad's health dramatically deteriorated. And towards the end of January, he was at the end of his life. My nana was pushing hard to get Grandad home.

My mum had taken leave from work and was spending every day with my nana at the nursing home. I would go down when I could around having Frankie. I felt I should have gone more, but it became a place unsuitable for a baby.

On February 2nd 2022, my beloved grandad took his final breath. My poor nana had horrifically lost her son. Then she lost her husband, who she so desperately wanted to get home for his final days, all within eleven months of each other.

My nan and mum had missed my grandad passing by about forty minutes or so, even though they had been there all day.

Right after we got the news, we headed to the nursing home, and I met my nan and mum down there.

The second dead body I had seen.

I said my goodbyes, sobbing onto him. It was heartbreaking. I hugged my nan and mum and left them to say theirs.

Again, Mum and I were constantly at Nan's for the next week or so. I would take Frankie with me and he helped lift the mood.

A date was set for my grandad's funeral. It was also the start date for my new job; of course it was. The funeral was tough, but it felt comforting knowing that my grandad was back with his son. My mum and my nan were terrific, the strongest of women.

My new boss was fantastic and gave me my first day off on compassionate leave. I originally thought that I would have to change my start date.

Returning to work was like coming back to some sort of normality. The job worked around us as a family and paid a good wage. I worked only three days a week, but it was enough.

However, midwifery was still very prominent in my mind. No job felt like it would be enough for me, and I was desperate to chase my dream.

And so I did.

In April 2022, I had been continuously bleeding vaginally on and off weekly from when I began taking my contraceptive pill back in the October of 2021, eight months prior.

I had contacted the GP several times regarding this, probably on four separate occasions. Still, I kept getting the same response every time: my body was adjusting. I knew my body, and I knew that something wasn't right. Even though it was changing back to pre-pregnancy, my gut was telling me that something more was going on.

But I was so drained and paranoid at this point because of the HPV they kept on finding on my smear test. I demanded that the doctor check what was going on. I went to the GP, and they examined me vaginally using a speculum. She told me that she found a cyst growing on my cervix, which was more than likely caused by the contraceptive pill. *Oh, that is just peachy!*

She told me to come back in two months to see if it had gone as she said it could sometimes happen. I was to carry on taking the pill as it's apparently nothing to worry about.

...

In May 2022, we went to Majorca on our first family holiday as a three. It was a much-needed break from everything. Even though we were never off duty as we had our nine-month-old with us, it was brilliant to play with him in the water and have some proper family time together.

I can't say that my mental health was thriving again, but I was in a significantly better place than I had been eight months prior.

I told Jake that I needed to give midwifery a go. I needed to try for myself. I wanted more out of my working life and to go further. That had a significant impact on my mental state because I am someone who strives for more and is eager to do so. I had learnt that about myself over the previous four years or so. What happened to my Uncle Kev made me want to chase my dreams more.

Jake had come to terms with the fact that this was what I wanted and that I wasn't ready for more children anytime soon. I think that, by the time we were having this conversation (which didn't get resolved around eight months prior), he realised that I was nowhere near ready to have more children. I was still learning how to navigate parenting and postnatal hormones with the one that I had! And he was brilliant. He was and still is my biggest cheerleader.

Also, one of the most significant moments in my life happened on that holiday to Majorca.

We woke up early one morning, well, like every morning, because that's what having a nine-month-old on holiday is like; it was not *relaxing*.

Breakfast opened at 8 am in the hotel, and Jake suggested that we go for a walk along the seafront. Little did I know that there was a game plan behind this.

We went back to the hotel and had breakfast. I told Jake that I was going back to the room to brush my teeth and use the toilet. I left him downstairs, finishing up feeding Frankie. About twenty minutes later, he sent me a message.

Jake:
Are you making your will up there?

Sarcastic shit. I chuckled to myself and told him that I wouldn't be long. I had become too engrossed in my mate's group chat, which was pinging off like it often does about some random topic.

I got sorted and went downstairs.

He told me that he was going to brush his teeth. He then suggested that Frankie and I wait for him downstairs and go to the beach that morning before it got busy. That sounded like a good plan!

Frankie had fallen asleep in his pram by the time we got there. *Brilliant; we can relax for half an hour or so,* is what I had thought.

We set our towels down on the sun loungers that we had chosen at the front of the beach. It was near enough empty, with just a few people on sun loungers further down and a few people on their morning walks. It was so peaceful.

Jake told me that he wanted a photo of me looking out into the ocean before I got comfy. I didn't think anything of it and began walking to the water.

I was walking towards the sea with him behind me, and I half-turned around to ask if this was far enough, but he quickly told me to keep going.

I took a few more steps forward - *we were still very close to our sleeping baby* - and Jake said, "Jazz."

I turned around and saw that he was down on one knee, holding a ring box with the most beautifully breathtaking ring.

He asked, "Will you marry me?"
WHAT!!!!!!
Oh my god, oh my god, oh my god!

I stood there for what felt like forever to Jake. My hands were to my mouth, and I was in complete shock.

He ended up saying, "Well, will you?"

I giggled with tears in my eyes and said, "Of course I will!"

It was the most beautiful moment, perfect in fact. I remember thinking that it could not have been any better.

We were on a high. It was some fantastic news to tell the family after the shit circumstances that we had encountered in the last year or so. I couldn't wait to start planning our wedding, and it didn't take me long before I got to it when we were home.

...

But, in the back of my mind, I couldn't stop thinking about the cyst that the GP had found, mainly because I was bleeding on that holiday, too.

In June 2022, I went back to the same GP who had seen me two months before to check the situation of my cyst. She examined me again, but this time, she sounded concerned. She said that the cyst had grown in size when she expected it to have gone. She told me that she needed to refer me to the gynaecologist at the hospital for further investigation but also reassured me that it wasn't likely anything to worry about.

How could I not worry?

I have had two positive HPV smear tests, and her face was telling a different story.

Also, she told me not to be alarmed, but she was referring me to the two-week cancer pathway to be seen quickly.

Yeah, I'm calm...

Every bad scenario went through my fragile mind. I was going to die. Frankie would have to grow up without a mum. Jake would be a single parent struggling.

The doctor told me that, in the meantime, to either stop taking the pill or double my dose to see if it would stop the bleeding. I thought that doubling my dose was a horrific idea, so I said that I would just come off the pill.

I received my letter in the post days later, with an appointment date precisely two weeks later. I was so nervous; it was all I could think about.

The day before my appointment, I felt like I had hit rock bottom. I suddenly was so emotional that I couldn't talk to anyone. I was such a bitch to Jake, bless him. I was so scared that they might have to take a biopsy or, worse, tell me that it's cancer or, *even* worse, take a biopsy, *then* tell me it's cancer!

The appointment day had come, and I dropped Frankie off with Jake's dad before I went. On the way, my mind was going at a thousand miles per hour and I couldn't slow it down. But, oddly, I didn't feel as low as I had the day before.

I wasn't in the waiting room long before they called me in, which I was thankful for.

I saw a lovely gynaecologist. He listened to my concerns about the pill and the HPV that had shown positive on the two previous smear tests. He told me about his frustration with my GP practice, saying that they should have investigated sooner and not just kept telling me that it was my body getting used to it.

I told him about how low I had been feeling the day before. And about how I've been bleeding more times than not over the last eight months. He examined me and told me that my cyst had burst, which he believed to have happened the day before. He said that it was probably why I was feeling so depressed, as the pill made the cyst. Hormones were feeding it like a depressant, as if my body was rejecting it. So, when it burst, the hormones were released into my body.

I think that's how he described it, anyway. I wish I had recorded what he said, but it was along those lines.

He checked for cancerous cells but couldn't detect any. He told me that the HPV was still present but wasn't threatening and then said I only needed three-yearly smears.

Phew! What a relief!

He also told me to take a break from contraception for six months to give my body a break.

He chuckled when I told him that I'd tell Jake we'd been banned from sex for six months for a laugh.

He jokingly said, "Don't do that; he will be putting in a complaint!"

Funny guy.

...

A job opportunity arose within the same NHS trust I was working for but within the community nursing team. I thought that this would help me gain some good baseline transferable clinical skills and help me with the university application process. I applied for it and got the job. I was also starting to plan our wedding at this point.

In June 2022, I started my new senior healthcare support worker role in the community nursing team. This role entailed medicine management for administering insulin, enoxaparin and vitamin B12 injections. I also took blood samples and attended to wound care. I loved it, and it put me in a good position to get where I wanted to be.

Next, I still needed to take an access course to higher education, equivalent to three A-Levels or something similar.

However, I decided that the best option for me would be to do it through an online learning centre, fitting it around my family and work life. I could do it in my own time, within reason. I planned to complete my work in the evening when Frankie was in bed and it was more flexible than going to college. The beauty of it was that you only did one subject at a time, rather than all three at once, so it wasn't hugely overwhelming.

We planned to pay for the monthly option that the learning centre offered for the access course, but my mum told me to speak to Little Nana because she wanted to help me. I did, and she paid for the course for me; she was amazing. I couldn't let her down.

...

In July 2022, we celebrated Frankie's first birthday. It was a lovely day. We had a party in the garden at our house, and all of our family and friends joined. He was exceptionally spoiled! I couldn't believe that he was already one, but I also couldn't believe where the last year of my life had gone.

I also completed my enrolment in the course and began to plod my way through it. The first four modules were ungraded, and thank God they were. I wasn't getting the grades I needed, and I remember thinking, "I don't know how I will ever do this."

It was all assignment-based. I hadn't done assignments since school, twelve years prior. They also required referencing, something that I had never done, and that's where I lost a lot of marks and didn't give enough depth.

I began to think that maybe I wasn't cut out for it at all. My online tutor gave me some good pointers for referencing and ideas to deepen my critical thinking. Regarding science modules, which were also assignment-formatted, she advised me on textbooks that I could order that were helpful with my learning level. I felt more confident after my conversation with my tutor about tackling the final ungraded module.

And then, my heart was about to break again.

In August 2022, I was just about to begin the last ungraded module of the access course.

My nana had to go to the hospital because she had fallen and fractured her wrist. She stayed in because she was dehydrated and needed extra care. I think that she was in for nearly two weeks, maybe just under.

After Jake had proposed to me, we planned to have our engagement party on August 20th. The date was chosen around the families' busy lives so that everyone could attend.

However, my nana was due to be discharged from the hospital that day, and my mum was on hand to pick her up, so she wasn't drinking.

It was pretty late in the day, and my nana was still waiting for the relevant paperwork to be done before she could go home. Finally, my mum got to the call to get her. She dropped her at home and helped get her settled for the night.

Sunday 21st August 2022.

I got a phone call from my mum at about 10 am saying that Little Nana was struggling to breathe and that she was just waiting for an ambulance.

Jake was at work, so I phoned his sister, who came immediately to watch Frankie for me while I went over.

I had a clinical observation kit in my car from my community nursing role. I did a set of observations on her, and everything was mainly within normal parameters from what I can remember, but her pulse was relatively high. However, her oxygen levels were acceptable, considering she sounded like she couldn't fill her lungs.

The ambulance came not long after and repeated them. They were unsure as to what was causing the breathing issues, and then they told my nan that they needed to take her in for further investigation. And, right then, I saw my nana give up. Going back into the hospital was the last thing that she wanted.

Once they had gotten Nan into the ambulance, she looked at me with her oxygen mask on and mimicked blowing me a kiss.

I blew one back and said, "I'll see you soon, Nan. Love you."

Mum went in the ambulance with my nan. However, they initially wouldn't let her in due to the COVID restrictions still in place, but people requiring extra support were allowed to have a chaperone. I went home, and Jake was back from work at this point, and his sister had gone.

I waited to hear from my mum all day as I couldn't visit; Nana was getting progressively worse with each update.

At around 14:00, my mum called me and told me that the family was to come at the doctor's desecration. And we all knew what that meant. *Not again.*

I wasn't ready for another death yet. Especially not my precious Little Nana. None of us were. But then, can you ever be prepared for someone to die? *I don't think so.*

We dropped Frankie at Jake's mum's around the corner and drove to the hospital.

Jake dropped me off at the door and then went to find a parking space. I was shown to the room that my nan was in; it was a resuscitation room.

My stepdad was already there with my mum. Nana was unconscious, and it looked like she was gasping for breath. It was horrible to see, and my heart shattered. Auntie Yvette, my cousins and my sister arrived; Jake had already joined by this point.

We all stayed for hours. We were holding her hand and having our final words with her.

I had been in such a hurry to get to the hospital that I hadn't brought any sanitary products that I needed!

Fuck's sake!

Being a woman can be so inconvenient!

I had also forgotten to bring a jumper, and I was getting chilly. As we don't live far from the hospital, Jake and I went home to get a change of clothes and sort ourselves out. We hadn't eaten either, so we planned to grab a sandwich and head straight back.

Before we left, I remember seeing Jake kiss my poor little nana on her forehead, saying his goodbyes. That pulled on my heartstrings. Everyone left the room for us to do so, just in case we missed her passing. I told Jake to leave me alone with my nan, and he waited outside.

I told her that I wouldn't be long and asked if she could hold on until I got back because I wanted to hold her hand whilst she went. I kissed her hand and said goodbye.

About ten minutes later, my sister called, and I knew what she was going to say.

Only two minutes after I had left, she had passed away.

I was so angry at myself. Why hadn't I just waited another two minutes? I had been there five hours; what was another *two minutes*? Why was the universe punishing me? I was so emotionally furious.

I had just managed to sort out my sanitary issue before my sister phoned. We then quickly returned to the hospital.

When we arrived, my mum, her cousin, my sister, auntie, stepdad and my sister's fiancée stood by her bed. My cousins had to leave because of childcare issues. It must have been so hard for them to say goodbye to Nana that day and Grandad earlier in the year after everything with their dad; my uncle.

When I saw my nana, I broke, and I had lost all strength in my body as I crumbled to the floor. I could feel my insides being torn apart. I sobbed, and my stepdad came and helped me up whilst hugging me.

I went over to my nan and told her that we'd had a deal. She was going to wait. My mum and auntie said that they thought she had waited for me to go. I wept whilst I held my forehead to hers, telling her that I was so glad that she was back with her beloved husband and son and that I would see her again one day. I told her to visit and I'm sure that she has done.

Sleep tight, my angel.

We left my mum in the room to say goodbye to her in private. Even though I don't know what was said, we could see her through the window in the door, and it was the most heart-wrenching scene to witness.

When we all left the hospital, an elderly man approached us with his son behind him. His son was desperately encouraging his dad to go back inside the hospital, pleading, even.

The elderly man was obviously mentally unwell and confused. He made eye contact with me, and I grabbed his attention quickly and began talking to him. I held out my arm for him to link to, and I walked him back into the hospital while chatting away to him. His son was behind us, directing me.

Once I had walked with him to where he needed to be, he settled onto his bed, and his son turned to thank me. He was so grateful. He looked mentally and physically exhausted like he had been caring for his father for a long while.

He said that he could tell that we had just either had terrible news or lost someone from how we were all crying while standing in the car park, saying goodbye to each other when his dad approached us. He gave me his sympathies for us and thanked me again. It was the most surreal encounter straight after my nan dying.

Days later, I was still so emotional. It was the first time that my mum felt like she didn't have to be strong for anyone else. So did I.

There was no filling our days with distraction after this death at my grandparent's house. We just grieved.

I briefly considered giving up the access course. I felt like I was setting myself up to fail; I wasn't academic enough for it, let alone for university.

But I didn't quit. I wasn't going to let my nana down.

Chapter 12
Lost in Torment

"Grief comes in two parts. The first is loss. The second is the remaking of life." (Rophie, 2008)

On September 1st 2022, I filled out my UCAS application for university. I applied to three but wanted only the one closest to me because I have a child. The other two were for interview experience if it were to work out that way.

The graded parts of my course had also begun. I was on my first module, *Biology: Anatomy and Physiology of the Human Muscles and Skeleton*. It is a complex topic. I had no idea how to complete it, let alone get the grade that I needed. It was a scary thought, but I plodded through. I worked really hard to teach myself the content.

A few days after handing it in, I was at work, just coming out of a patient's house. I got an email saying that my first graded module was back and worth three credits (I'll explain the credit part next).

I felt my heart begin to beat fast. I didn't dare look but I was also eager to.

Oh God.

I got in the car and logged in; I got a distinction!
OH MY GOD!

I was so pleased! I rang Jake and my mum and texted my mate's group chat. Everyone was buzzing for me!

Getting that grade gave me hope that I could achieve what I thought was impossible; it spurred me on. My angels were looking down on me. *Thank you Nan, Grandad and Kev.*

My access course worked by assigning each module either six or three credits. I had to take five biology, three sociology and two psychology modules; which amounted to forty-five credits. *It's complicated, I know.*

Each module was graded according to distinction, merit, pass or fail. For example, a six-credit assignment graded at distinction would mean six distinctions for that module.

The UCAS points required for midwifery at the university I wanted to attend were one hundred and twenty. That equated to twenty-four credits worth of distinctions and twenty-one credits worth of merits.

I did my work mainly in the evenings when Frankie was in bed, as planned.

...

Thursday, September 15th 2022, was the day we lay my beautiful Little Nana to rest. It was a tough day to get through, but we did it. My mum gave a lovely speech, just like she had at her brother's and dad's funeral. *What a woman!* Honestly, she is so strong. I hope that I have at least half of the strength inside me as she has.

The following day was one of the best days of my life. My cousin came over from America to attend Nan's funeral. He stayed in the States when my aunt and uncle moved back, along with my other two cousins.

He was also a huge plane enthusiast like me and was nearly a qualified pilot, so he arranged for us to go flying. *It was a dream come true!*

I love planes; they are a remarkable piece of machinery. That was my other dream job: being a pilot! But I am not clever enough for that. But who knows? I'm full of surprises!

We went flying at Sturgate near Gainsborough. It was incredible. The instructor was brilliant. He was a retired high-ranking RAF pilot who had let me take control of the plane for ages. It was a brilliant day after such an emotional one the day before.

But then it was like everyone went away.

Jake turned thirty that year and was going on a five-day golfing holiday with his dad, his friend and his friend's dad.

Two days after the funeral, my mum went on a much-needed two-week holiday, and Jake's mum and sister also went away for a few days. I suddenly felt very alone. I had to take time off work as my childcare was away at the same time as everyone else. It was just Frankie and me; I felt envious that we couldn't escape normality following the funeral.

...

At the start of November 2022, Jake and I went away for a weekend over which bonfire night fell on. Frankie stayed with Jake's parents, and we had a relaxing time, which was exactly what I needed. I was still grieving for the loss of my nan. Well, all the family members we had lost in the last eighteen months. I was trying to come to terms with it all, even the miscarriage we had was spoken about.

We stayed in a lodge about forty minutes from home. It had a hot tub, and we could watch the fireworks from it. It was perfect.

On the Saturday, we went for a long, refreshing walk and a nice pub lunch. Then, we spent the rest of that day in the hot tub until the evening, when more fireworks began. It was a nice break from parenting, work, and my access course.

I was due to have a GP appointment on Monday to go back on contraception following my appointment with the gynaecologist, who had recommended a six-month break. It wasn't quite half a year yet, but I felt ready to give it a go again.

However, whilst we were on our weekend away, we got carried away, and a condom was not used. We immediately went to the pharmacy for emergency contraception.

For God's sake…

I was honest with the pharmacist and said that we got carried away. It was like the police were questioning me after committing a crime.

On Monday, when I had my appointment at the GP for contraception, I explained what had happened; *I basically held my hands up and confessed.* She told me not to worry, and I did the right thing by getting the emergency contraception. She advised me to do a pregnancy test in a few weeks and then prescribed me a different pill from what I had previously been on.

Admittedly, I forgot to do the advised pregnancy test.

When we were back to normality, I continued to wait apprehensively to hear back from the universities that I had applied to. It felt like torture, not knowing if all the hard work I was putting in was for nothing.

The following week, I got an email from my first-choice university inviting me to an interview the very next week!

OH, LORD!!

I didn't have long to prepare. I had to choose an article out of the six given to discuss at my interview; I picked one about maternity services in Norway. I can't remember its content, but I found it the most interesting, which gave me more confidence in talking about it.

I was so nervous about the interview. It was done online via Teams, and five other people were interviewed at the same time. I had done so much background reading and practising by answering questions I knew would be asked, such as "Why do you want to be a midwife?"

"I want to be a midwife because there is no other job that I know could fill me with the same sense of reward, like supporting women through the most vulnerable, yet life-changing, experience. To provide the empowerment all families deserve to transition into parenthood. I want to educate both women and men about the whirlwind changes that happen to females' bodies antenatally, intrapartum and postnatally because I believe knowledge is key to resulting in positive outcomes." I'm sure my answer was something along those sorts of lines.

The interview lasted nearly two hours. I remember being absolutely bursting for a wee, but I tried to play it cool because I was on camera.

I came away from the interview, not wholly sure how I felt about it at all. I had done my absolute best but couldn't tell if I had done well *enough*. I did as well as I could with six other people interviewing simultaneously, and it often felt like I was copying others' answers when it was my turn to speak.

They told us that we would hear within a couple of weeks if we were successful or not. It was so nerve-racking. I checked my emails a million times a day, even the day that I was interviewed, including junk mail and everything.

On the 24th of November, only two days following my interview, I heard back from the university. I had been at work, having just finished my penultimate visit for the day. I got in my car and felt my heart sink into my stomach when I opened the email.

Dear Applicant,

Thank you for participating in the midwifery interview recently. Unfortunately, you did not meet the threshold.

However, we would like to offer you an alternative conditional offer for either adult nursing or mental health nursing. Please would you let me know by 1 December 2022 regarding which field you would be interested in?

I sobbed my heart out in my car. Everything that I had been doing was for nothing. I didn't want to be a nurse. I wanted to be a *midwife*. They are two very different roles, and I couldn't have spent three years studying (well, four years, including my access course) for a job I did not want. I must have been in my car at least half an hour before I decided to drive to my next patient's house whilst pulling myself together.

Deep breaths, come on.

My next patient was an elderly gentleman that I had never met before. I was thankful for this as he didn't know that I was usually in a better mood. I attended to the wounds on his legs that required undressing, cleansing and re-bandaging, so I was there for about thirty minutes. He was lovely, distracted me from my miserable self and told me interesting tales of his life. He also shared a love for aircraft, and we bonded over that. He was shocked when I told him that I had flown a plane, and I was slightly smug by that.

I finished redressing his legs, said goodbye to him and headed home to document my morning visits and cry while I did it.

I could have gone back to the office, where most of the team goes in the afternoon, to catch up, write their notes, and socialise. I did not want to be social. I just wanted to wallow in self-pity by myself.

I had already told Jake about the news of not getting into midwifery at the only university I could have realistically attended. He was so supportive and suggested nursing as an option, as I had mentioned that I could go on to do an eighteen-month 'top-up' course to be a midwife from a nurse. *Bless him.* I said that I would have to think about it.

We had already found the perfect wedding venue but hadn't booked it. Jake suggested that we go out for tea and book our wedding to cheer me up. My mum came and babysat Frankie while we went out that evening. Booking our wedding was exciting and made me happy. However, I still felt heavily defeated by the result of my interview.

My mum worked from my house to look after Frankie for me the next day. He wasn't feeling great, so I spent most of my working morning with him at the doctor's and then at the pharmacy, getting his antibiotics for a chest infection. My boss was great, but they were really short-staffed and vital visits were needed. She only gave me three as I had a poorly boy at home and was running behind.

Once I had finished sorting Frankie and got him settled on the sofa with his first dose of antibiotics and a packet of digestives for him and my mum to share, I went off to do my visits.

In the car, I was mulling over everything.

Do I do nursing?

Do I call them and ask for feedback or give up?

The job I was already doing was great, and I loved it, but I knew that it wasn't enough for me.

I wasn't going to give up.

I couldn't give up.

I couldn't let Little Nana down.

I pulled up to my last patient of the day. I sat in the car and phoned the university's main reception, who put me through to midwifery admissions. They didn't answer, so I left a voicemail. I told them my name and that I wanted to talk more in-depth about my options with nursing and how it could get me to my ultimate goal of being a midwife because that is where my passion is.

I then went into my last visit, which wasn't long; it was just a dressing on an arm that needed replacing.

When I came back to my car, I checked my phone, and I found an email from the university.

Hi Jasmine,

I hope you are well. I just wanted to contact you to apologise. I believe my colleague contacted you to say you had been unsuccessful in your midwifery interview and were offered adult nursing instead.

There appears to be some confusion; unfortunately, you were contacted in error. I can confirm that you performed very well in your interview and that we would like to make you an offer to study midwifery.

I have contacted Student Admin today to update your UCAS application to reflect this offer, so hopefully, you will receive confirmation very soon.

I'm really sorry for any stress or upset this error may have caused. I can assure you that you have successfully obtained a conditional offer.

OH MY GOD!

I had to pinch myself and read it out loud to believe that I wasn't dreaming. I called Jake and squealed down the phone to him, something along the lines of, "I got in!" But it was all just a high-pitched noise to him; I managed to calm down slightly and explain.

I went home, where my mum was lying on the sofa with Frankie, and I told her she was over the moon, beaming with excitement for me. Frankie had perked up a little by the time I was home, and he was even joining in on the excited vibes.

I told everyone, and it felt amazing to share the news! I was proud of myself for getting this far. Now, all I needed to do was get the grades for the conditions of my offer.

I did well and got the grades throughout my biology unit. From September to December 2022, I completed all the biology modules back-to-back. I got distinctions in everything, equating to twenty-four; all the distinctions I needed! I was learning and taking in each module's content because I wanted to understand it. *It felt good to learn.*

I did have a two-week break over Christmas 2022 from my course.

And things turned to shit again.

The next bad thing to happen... That's what my life was feeling like— a waiting game for the next person to die or a shit thing to happen.

December 20th 2022.

When I was prescribed my contraceptive pill six weeks prior, the GP had advised me to take one every day for nine weeks and have a four-day break to prevent ovulation; she said that women can still ovulate within the seven-day break.

I had been on this style of pill years ago, long before I got pregnant and before I began the mini one you take every day without a break.

I am not entirely sure why she advised me to do it this way. Maybe it was because of the issues I had before. However, I wasn't going to question her. It was the pill that women usually take for twenty-one days and then have a seven-day break. So I did as she said.

I had been feeling emotional and ratty, but I put that down to everything that my family had been through and the hard work that I was putting into my course.

On the evening of December 20th, Jake asked me if he could go golfing on Boxing Day. We were going to Liverpool the day after Boxing Day with his family between Christmas and New Year. I thought that the 26th would be the day that we would get packed and sorted.

I flew off the handle. I was so irrational. In one breath, I would apologise for being such a bitch and the next, I would become angry all over again, saying that it's family time, etc. Which, I can't lie... golf can happen *anytime*. Boxing Day cannot.

Half of me thought that I was being totally irrational because I had lost a lot of my family and wanted to make it still feel like a family day.

I was also having huge cramping pain in my lower abdomen which had been there for a few days. I thought that my period must have broken through the pill as I still had three weeks left before I was having a break. I went to bed a mardy bitch and poor Jake just took my miserable mood and told me that it was okay; he wouldn't go.

Then I felt terrible and told him that he could go and that I was just overreacting.

What was this pill doing to me?

I'm being so horrible.

Poor Jake couldn't win.

I took some painkillers and put a sanitary pad on because I felt like it was coming; then I went to bed.

I woke up the following day and I had begun bleeding in the night.

I went downstairs to the bathroom to get ready for work. I sat in the toilet to take my sanitary pad off and then I saw it; everything clicked in my mind.

I was miscarrying. Again... *I think.*

I looked at the little prawn-shaped figure of a fetus that had come out of me for ages; I was inspecting it.

I had just learned about embryology in my reproductive module for my course, and it looked exactly like the diagram of a 5 to 6-week-old fetus. I could see little blood vessels running through its pasty transparent colour.

And then what felt like a massive blood clot fell out of me. I looked at it and I knew that it was the placenta.

Jake was up and with me in the bathroom and I said, "I think that's our baby."

He was so confused and so was I. We both had tears in our eyes. He went to the shop and got me a pregnancy test and I phoned into work and told them what had happened; or, what I thought was happening.

I did the test, and it said it was negative. *What is going on?* All of the signs pointed to being pregnant with the mood swings. I had been the same when I was pregnant with Frankie. Also, what had come out of me resembled what had come out in the first miscarriage.

But how?

Oh, wait!

The weekend away!

The emergency contraception works by delaying or preventing ovulation. What if I was already going through it?

Frankie was staying at Jake's mum's house the night before anyway as I had an early appointment at the foot clinic for an annoying and persistently ingrown toenail. I went with Jake to the appointment as he had taken the day off after what we both saw in my sanitary pad.

I made an *AskMyGP* request and sent photos of what I had expelled, explaining my contraception story of late.

I got a reply over the messenger part of the app when I requested a phone call. It was a different doctor than who I had seen for my contraception appointment. They told me that I couldn't have been pregnant if the test was negative. And that was it. They completed my request before I could send a reply.

They did not explain what the massive blood clot could be or the prawn-shaped thing with blood vessels that came out of me. I was actively bleeding heavily (when I wasn't supposed to due to the pill) and they offered no sort of reassurance or care.

I was so angry and confused; I needed some answers. I know my body. My gut was telling me that I was miscarrying. Everything was just like what I had experienced before.

I rang the private scan clinic that we had used previously to see if she could provide some information; I told her everything.

She was as lovely as ever. She explained that everyone is different and that no one is 'textbook'. People's bodies can reject things so quickly. From what I described, she thought that I had begun miscarrying a few days earlier due to the pain that I was experiencing. My body only released the fetus that morning which would be why the pregnancy test showed negative. It had come away from my uterine wall and had been sitting in my uterus, waiting for my body to expel it.

That's how she explained it.

I was so pleased that she had helped me. It wasn't like I was glad that I was miscarrying but at least it added up and made sense. If it wasn't a miscarriage and the pill had caused that to come out of me, I would never have taken it again after this ordeal was complete.

The GP let me down. They made me feel silly like I was overreacting, and they didn't care. I was so angry at how they made me feel so stupid, especially when I had experienced this before; but last time I knew that I was pregnant.

I began to feel so guilty.

I was guilty for not wanting to be pregnant and actively trying not to be when I was.

Guilty for taking the morning-after pill and relying on it.

Guilty of not doing the pregnancy test as I had been advised to by the GP.

And guilty of losing another baby.

It was getting too much.

Life was becoming a lot. It was beginning to feel like the streak of shit events was just never going to end.

While in Liverpool, Jake's mum and I had a heart-to-heart conversation. She suggested that I talk to a counsellor because I was losing myself and she could see it. Even though everything in my body was telling me to be defensive and say that I was okay, I knew that I wasn't fine at all. I hadn't been for a long time but I was sort of just accepting this was me now; anxiety-ridden.

Since having Frankie, I would have intrusive thoughts that something terrible was going to happen to him, Jake or me. I didn't say anything to anyone other than the odd remark to Jake.

I would have moments where I was scared to take Frankie out of the house on my own from the threat of everything. In my mind, my thought process would go from someone stealing him to a car mounting the pavement and killing him.

Months later, I still had these thoughts when I returned to work. I then began to get obsessed that I was going to crash and die whilst I was out on visits. I was also sure that Jake was going to do the same on his forty-minute commute to the farm. And Frankie would end up with no parents. I would automatically think of the worst scenario if I hadn't heard from Jake by a specific time. Still, even now, my mind sometimes goes there, but I feel like I have more control over my thought processes.

I had been living with anxiety since Frankie was born but it was getting progressively worse. It was probably because of all the bad shit that had been happening around me but also, being a new mum can play havoc with your anxiety levels.

When you become a mother, the world changes.

It's like in the wild; everything around you is a threat to your innocent, tiny cub and you're always on high alert to detect any danger. Things you wouldn't have given a second thought to before you became a mother are all of a sudden too scary to attempt. There becomes jeopardy in everything.

It's just learning to control it rationally.

I told Jake's mum that I would go to see a therapist; she even offered to pay privately for me but I told her not to worry. I would sort it out.

We returned from our Liverpool trip the day before New Year's Eve 2022. I went to see my mum to tell her that I would find a counsellor to talk to. She was supportive of the idea.

I don't know how, after everything she had been through in such a short space of time, she kept on going every day. She just powered through and still does.

Things hadn't been great with my stepdad's mental health around that Christmas period. It was like a delayed grief for his father had caught up with him after we lost my uncle in such a horrific way soon after his father died.

I admire my mum so much. She is resilient and full of life. She has had to learn a new way of living with how she lost her brother and then lost her parents. And before all of that, she had nearly lost her daughter when my sister had an ectopic pregnancy and was rushed into emergency surgery; that's when her mental health began to struggle. *It was a scary time.*

She has her down days but the good ones outweigh the bad. All these events have changed her over the last few years; it's like she appreciates life more and takes advantage of opportunities that she wouldn't have before, whether in her career, home or social life. Most importantly, she is taking time for herself. I respect that woman in every single way. She has supported me through everything, even during her own troubles. She is my true hero.

Keep on smashing life, mum.

On New Year's Eve 2022, Jake's parents were having their annual party at their house, and Frankie was staying over. Jake's mum agreed not to drink and to be the responsible adult for him.

My mum and stepdad weren't coming to the party due to my stepdad's poor mental health at that time. He was only just beginning to really grieve for his father, who he had lost just before my uncle committed suicide all those months ago. However, he found help with the fantastic *Andy's Man Club* charity organisation that supports male mental health. He really has overcome some tough days and I couldn't be prouder.

On the night of the party, Jake went to the pub around the corner for a drink with his mates before joining later on, and he left his phone at his mum's house.

I put Frankie down to sleep upstairs before everyone arrived but, while getting him ready for bed, he was sick, a *lot*. It was only because he had drunk his milk too fast but that shot my anxiety levels through the roof.

Here we go again.

Jake's mum and I sorted him out. I got him settled, put him down in his cot to sleep and put on the baby monitor; the world's shittiest baby monitor that doesn't give a clear picture and loses signal equates to an anxious mother.

We went downstairs and people started arriving. I tried to relax and engage in conversation but I couldn't hold much of one. The kitchen started filling with more people by the minute and I became extremely anxious. Jake's uncle asked me if I was okay and I burst out crying. I was holding onto the baby monitor and constantly watching it because I couldn't hear anything besides music and people. I was scared that he was going to be sick again or choke and I couldn't hear him. It was like my body was filled with dread and I couldn't let go of it.

I began to feel panicky and like I couldn't breathe. I needed to get Frankie and go. Jake's mum and sister tried to calm me down but, at that moment, I just needed to get my baby and go home away from everyone. I couldn't even call Jake to tell him I was leaving.

I got sleepy Frankie out of bed. I felt bad for waking him, but I put him in the car and drove the two-minute ride home. I hadn't drunk anything.

As soon as we got home, he went straight back to sleep when I put him in bed. Afterwards, I went downstairs and sobbed.

What was happening to me?

It was like I couldn't keep up with my mind going ten to a dozen. But I did feel calmer now that I was at home and it was quiet; I could hear my baby if he needed me. Not that I didn't think Jake's mum wouldn't have been on high alert for him; my brain was just telling me that I needed to take him and myself to a calmer place. As a mother, you can never really relax when your children are around anyway, even if you are not 'on duty'.

Jake phoned me and I told him to stay at the party as I was going to bed very shortly. He was concerned but, in all honesty, I just wanted to be on my own. I needed rest. I felt so emotionally overwhelmed and drained from the pace that my thoughts were travelling at that I just needed to block it out with sleep; alcohol was definitely NOT what I needed! I had a cup of tea and then went to bed.

The following day, I woke up, and Jake was in bed. He had come home after the party while I was sleeping, but I half expected him to have stayed at his mum's, drunk and passed out. I took advantage of that fact and went for an early morning run in an attempt to straighten my head out. I ensured that he was fit enough to look after our little boy and not too hungover. Maybe that was mean of me, but I needed the fresh air.

I knew that I needed to do something about my mental health but I felt like I had no idea how to unscramble this brain of mine that was tormenting me. I felt like I had a brain block and didn't know how to complete the rest of my course.

A few days later, I began looking for a counsellor and found one relatively close to me. I booked a session with her, scheduled for the following week, and I began preparing for my first session.

Chapter 13
Found in Freedom

"It's hard to dance with the devil on your back, so shake him off." - Florence & The Machine's Shake It Out.

In January 2023, about two weeks before my first therapy session, I was going out with my friend for her birthday meal. We went into town and had some fantastic food and a few proseccos. Her sisters came as well and we had a great time.

My friend told her partner that she would be back in the early evening to spend the rest of her day with him so we shared a taxi as she only lives in the next village.

Jake was with Frankie at his mum's, having Sunday lunch like we all usually do. I had already eaten so I decided to go to the pub around the corner from his mum's to watch the football. Manchester United were playing, my team. We didn't get the football at our house because we didn't have the channels; so, the pub it was.

When I got there, I was met with the regular faces. Everyone knows everyone in our village so I had no issue going in to watch the football on my own. I got my drink and sat with the other punters. We played pool and the winner stayed on, like I usually would when we went to the local boozer.

I never make an effort to watch the footie at the pub. I usually wear leggings and baggy T-shirts; loungewear—the tomboy never left me.

But, because I had been out with my friends before, some of the regulars, both men and women, commented that I looked nice and scrubbed up well; they were just being friendly.

Another regular joined further into the game and said to me, "Jazz, where's Jake? Have you left him at home babysitting?" Of course, this was all in jest but my silly mind began to go into overdrive. *Not again....*

Jake knew that I was at the pub. I had texted him, asking him to pick me up when he finished his Sunday roast and take me home.

He had said, "There's ages left of the football yet, babe?" I just said that I needed to go home.

He had absolutely no issue with me being in the pub on my own. But I began to feel like I was doing something I shouldn't be; like I was being judged for being out without Jake. *So ridiculous!* I was literally feeling so guilty for being in my local pub, on my own, wearing make-up, a nice top and wet-look leggings. It wasn't as if I was wearing something revealing and it wasn't anyone else's fault that I was feeling that way; it was my own stupid mind that was becoming too much for me to handle.

Jake picked me up; I told him my thoughts and that I felt like I was doing something wrong. He was trying to reassure me. He must have found my irrational episodes draining because they became more regular. The prosecco probably didn't help my thought process but I also wasn't drunk either. I think that prosecco is the worst drink for me to induce 'beer fear' anxiety but it doesn't happen every time.

The next day, I woke up uncontrollably crying. Jake had already left for work by this time and Frankie was still asleep. I checked on him like I always did/do if I was awake before him because that is rare. And secondly, my anxious brain encouraged me too, but not so much anymore.

I was on the phone crying to Jake's younger of the two sisters. She encouraged me to speak to the doctor because it was time that I got the pills to help.

How did I get here?

How had I got to what felt like rock bottom?

The doctor booked me for an appointment with the mental health specialist in two days' time. It was a *long* two days. I had taken the week off work due to my mental state and I wish that I had just accepted the tablets the first time (which was sixteen months ago at this point).

Those last sixteen months could have been very different...

My appointment day had arrived. I divulged everything about my family trauma, my thought processes, my obsession with Jake, Frankie or me dying, my physical health, and how I felt I was becoming a burden for Jake because I was no longer the woman he fell in love with. I had become this anxious, irrational, irritable bitch, and I felt terrible for him. In my head, I felt like he was trapped with me because we had Frankie and he didn't know how to leave me.

He didn't feel that way at all but it would play on my mind. I would often say, "Be honest with me, won't you? If you ever fall out of love with me, just tell me." And then I would regret saying it because I thought those comments would push him away. I couldn't win. My *brain* would never let me win.

The mental health specialist told me that it sounded like I had experienced undiagnosed postnatal depression which had led to generalised anxiety disorder. Also, they wanted to refer me to the local therapy service '*Steps To Change*'. I said that I had my first session coming up the following week and I had booked it privately.

I was prescribed sertraline 50mg which they said to take only half a tablet a day for a week, then up it to a whole tablet. I never did that and I stayed at 25mg. I also stopped taking my contraceptive pill because I knew that it probably wasn't helping my mood either.

I began to have common side effects such as a faster heart rate and being awake at night. But they eased off after about four days.

I began to start my access course again after nearly a month off from just before my second miscarriage on December 21st 2022. I could try to focus again because the mental block towards my course was fading.

I began my counselling sessions, and they were beneficial. I told her everything that I had mentioned at the mental health specialist's appointment. She gave me some coping strategies and asked me to think of something that I love that I don't have any anxiety about. I said that I love cats and watching cute, funny cat videos online. That became my coping strategy when I began to feel anxious. I still use it now; Jake even reminds me to watch them.

When I would have intrusive thoughts of death or about how I thought that something terrible was going to happen, she taught me to be jovial with them and talk out loud to them by saying "Go away, you are not helpful today; thank you!" or "Oh, you again, fuck off, please." And then I would chuckle to myself.

I said that a lot at first but it gradually became less and less. I didn't have many sessions with her, only about four, but they were valuable ones and I took so much away from them. Being able to talk helped without someone trying to fix it for me with their opinions.

The human race is predominantly people-pleasers. We like to try to fix people's problems, even when they don't ask for an answer, and I'm guilty of that myself. However, sometimes, people just want/need to talk about what's troubling them without seeking answers or requiring someone's opinion. The best therapy can sometimes be just a set of ears to listen and a pair of arms to hug them. That alone can make a person feel more valid than trying to offer a solution all of the time, even if it seems irrational to you; it isn't to them. Just listen.

Over the months, my anxiety levels began to drop. I could drive around for work and the feeling of impending doom was reduced.

I joined a new gym with Jake's sister that had recently opened and was just over a five-minute drive from my house. I planned workouts around family life and booked into group classes. That also became like medicine; I needed them for their positive impact on my mental health and I still do. It's something that I enjoy, just like before I'd had Frankie, and I was ready to invest time into myself again.

I eventually finished my access course with forty-two distinctions and three merits; I couldn't believe it. After meeting their requirements, I received my place confirmation from my first-choice university.

I was so fucking proud of myself and I still am.

The access course obviously contributed to my stress levels because it was so intense. You have to do it around your work and family life. You weren't given allocated time for it like when you became a university student. I look back at that period of my life and wonder how I managed to get where I am today. But I could put that behind me and turn the page to a new way of living.

...

In April 2023, I thought that it would be best to go back on some form of contraception. I wanted to try the non-hormonal copper coil. I was booked on the three-month waiting list and, a week later, they phoned me to say that there had been a cancellation for later that day and I could take the spot if I wanted. So I did.

On my way, I was slightly nervous that it was going to hurt but I had given birth and had multiple checks of my cervix in the last year. I could fucking do this. *Easy*, I thought.

I went into the clinic room and they told me about the procedure, risks and side effects. I consented to go ahead but began to feel even more anxious.

I lay on the bed in the same position that you would for a smear test or vaginal examination: feet together and bring them to your bum. They proceeded and inserted the speculum to open my cervix which is never comfortable. Still, for the amount of time that they were trying to put the coil into my uterus, I think that I became fully dilated again.

The doctor said that it was awkward for them to get in. It wasn't overly painful but it began to feel toe-curlingly strange down there. I thought that I was going to throw up! Then, I felt my ears begin to ring, my skin came over all clammy and the colour drained from my face. *Great, this is how I die; having the coil fitted.* Okay, slight exaggeration.

After about half an hour of trying, they finally managed to get the coil in. *Hallelujah!* But I wasn't allowed to get up off the bed too soon because of my ghostly-looking skin. The doctor took my blood pressure which had dropped relatively low; they got me some water and I had to sit up slowly, then stand even slower.

How fucking dramatic can it get?

I thought that I would have to be admitted to the hospital at the rate that I was going.

After ten embarrassing minutes of theatrics, I got some colour back in my face and felt well enough to leave. It took a bloody long time for what is supposed to be a simple procedure. I must say, though, that it has been the best form of contraception I have ever used. On the one hand, it makes my periods heavier and more painful at times; I sometimes even have a bleed in between periods. However, it has been great not to have to use any contraception that is well-known for having a negative effect on a woman's mood. And for me, that's a winner.

I wonder one day if it will become equal between men and women on the hormonal-contraception front and if there will be a pill or injection invented for men to stop spermatogenesis temporarily and give women a goddamn break! *A-fucking-men.*

Life was becoming an enjoyment again. Not that I was ever living in full-blown depression or extreme anxiety where everything was too much. But I believe that I would have been heading that way if I hadn't had the support of my family, Jake's family and my friends. I did have episodes of what felt like torture inflicted on me from my brain. *Devil mind...* But I was strong enough not to let it win.

The mind can be the most dangerous weapon for its owner; my uncle was an unfortunate victim of his. It can play nasty tricks on you. All within a matter of seconds, it can send you thoughts of happiness and excitement, then fill you with ones of torment and doom that follow with a physical gut-wrenching feeling.

I was finding my old self again, the 'me' before all the shit. I was also learning how to navigate the new version of me; I was in a more relaxed, rational state of mind and my world felt calmer and became a pleasant place to live again. My anxiety levels dropped and it was almost as if breathing became an easier task to complete. Conversations seemed to be simpler and less of a chore and being a mum was becoming less of an anxiety-ridden part of my life. I began to view my relationship with Jake no longer as a ticking time bomb that would eventually have had enough of my emotional and erratic outbursts.

I still have times when anxiety creeps in and takes some pleasure away from my day but I have so much more control over myself now. It's all about knowing that it is common to not be on top of the world every day and also about being aware of balancing a normal state of emotions compared to an irrational state. Knowing yourself and knowing your triggers all before you reach breaking point is one of life's little games; unfortunately.

Everyone has their down days but I've finally learned that it is just part of 'normal' life.

Chapter 14
A New Path

A new challenge was fast approaching, a new path that would test, push and reward me.

After receiving acceptance to my place from the university, I told my community nursing manager. She congratulated and praised me for my hard work and for doing it around everything else in my life. She informed me that I would need to hand in my notice a month before I was due to start university.

I was on a summer 2023 countdown until I began, but it was also a summer of fun. Jake, Frankie and I went on a family holiday to Spain and had some much-needed quality time together. Two of my closest friends were pregnant and close in gestation, so I had two lovely baby showers to attend. Some of my friends were having their 30th birthday events, which meant that I, too, was getting one year closer to the big 3-0!

It was also one of my best friends' 30th birthdays. A few of her other friends and I went to Butlin's 90s Weekender; it was so much fun. I laughed so much at many moments over that weekend that my stomach muscles began hurting.

In July 2023, I went with my mum and Jake's mum to pick my wedding dress. It was such a magical day and an experience I will always remember. I also found the perfect dress in a little bridal boutique local to me— it was the first shop that I had been to.

It turned out to be a summer of social events, and I was finally in a mental state where I could properly enjoy such occasions again without overthinking every aspect of them.

However, there were times when occasions fell close together. I felt guilty for not being at home as much with Frankie or Jake while still working and attending my friend's celebrations. But, sometimes, it's just how things work out. And Jake never told me that I couldn't go. In fact, he encouraged me to go. He was getting the old Jazz back.

He wasn't missing out on all the fun. He also had his occasions with his friends and his golf days while working six days a week, so we were a busy family. Frankie wasn't left out either, and we would go on family days out to the beach, soft play, or to toddler-friendly adventure parks.

I was still working three days a week until starting university, so Frankie and I would spend two solid days together weekly.

I also had to work one in three weekends because that's the NHS for you. We often asked the family to have Frankie one morning on the weekend I *was* working, as Jake also had to work one day every weekend, but that's usually until dinner time.

I stayed on a bank contract with my community nursing team. I booked in some morning shifts in advance for a weekend in the October after I had begun uni as it's better money. And, keeping your foot in the door of your old job isn't such a bad thing when you're doing a uni degree that requires you to pass exams and assignments with only two chances. Otherwise, you have to either retake that module the following year with the next intake of students or leave the course; it's all very cut-throat. So, I thought picking up some bank shifts would be a smart move— a backup plan, so to speak.

Another thing that I didn't realise before becoming a student was that you get no help with childcare; the tax-free childcare that working parents get is taken away from you. And you have to pay the full amount— circumstantial, of course. Which also led to me doing more bank shifts. That is what happened to me and many others. I think it is barbaric, to say the least, when you are doing a full-time university degree on an NHS learner fund and a student finance loan.

It's not as if Jake earns a tremendous amount, and we had to be careful as we were also getting married the following year. Still, I'll explain how we managed to afford that in time. The bank shifts helped pay for the extra childcare charges we now had to face, and our parents were great. They helped out by looking after Frankie so we didn't have to put him into childcare full-time, just like they had when I went back to work part-time. We will both be forever grateful.

Anyway, I'm not here to slag off the government making these decisions.

September 2023 was the month I began following my dream. It was also the month Frankie started preschool. I remember his first day as if it were yesterday. When I dropped him off, I sobbed my heart out when I got home. I couldn't believe that my baby was now at preschool. He quickly adapted to his new surroundings and began to thrive developmentally. I couldn't be prouder of my boy; he really is a superstar.

A family friend of Jake's who also lives in the village told me that her daughter-in-law was also starting midwifery; she lived in the village, too!

I contacted her, and we met at the local pub for a drink to get to know each other better. Although we knew *of* each other, we had never actually *met*.

We planned to meet on Saturday evening before starting uni the following Monday. We got on really well, and I already knew her partner from socialising in the pub. He gets on great with Jake, too, and he's also known him a long time. There were no awkward silences; there was just great conversation and talking about how we thought the course would be.

She offered to pick me up and drive us both to university on Monday, and I was so glad that I already had a friend to walk in with. It wasn't long before we began biking to university together, as she is a fitness freak like me.

The first day was like any other day before starting something new: nerve-wracking and exciting. We met another girl who joined us, and we soon became inseparable. We quickly became good friends with another group of girls. It was all falling into place— *my uni family*.

Further down the line, the 'mum guilt' began to creep in, as expected. I was suddenly a full-time student with work to complete at home. Still, Jake and our families supported me in every way possible with that hurdle.

When I was growing up, my mum had to work; she needed to work to live. And that's what I was used to. It didn't make her a bad mother just because she wasn't always by my side. She often tells me to stop being so hard on myself when I mention the dreaded 'mum guilt'. My sister and I used to be in childcare and at either my dad's parent's or my mum's parent's house when ours were at work. It's just the way it was, but it didn't make us resent her or have a negative impact on our lives. We used to stay at our grandparents on our dad's side every Saturday night; that was our routine, and we loved being there.

I often look to Jake for reassurance that everything is okay and that I'm not missing out on too much with our son, but I suppose that is my anxious brain talking. It is not like I go for days without seeing him, but when I go on placement and work the long shifts, I sometimes miss him in the mornings and at night, but I do my best to make up time with him when I can.

I suppose every mother who becomes a student or has to return to work full-time often experiences 'mum guilt'. We live in a world that is so judgmental that it's hard not to question one's choices. I would love to change that narrative.

Mums cannot win. Society frequently penalises the ones who stay at home and labels them 'lazy' for not returning to work to look after their children. Then, those who do go back to work are judged for 'not wanting to spend time with their kids'. Then, the mothers, like many on my course, feel guilty for bettering themselves. It's a vicious cycle.

There is no real 'right time' to start university when you have a child. No matter their age, you will feel bad about missing out. I began university when Frankie was just over two years old, which worked for my little family and our parents, who helped make it possible. I know that not everyone has the luxury of family support, and I count myself as fortunate to be able to chase my dream because of them.

When women become mothers, it doesn't mean that our lives will stop. We are still who we were before, but with an addition. We don't always get it right, and there can be a lot of trial and error, but we live and learn. No one is perfect; we just do our best.

...

After the Christmas period in 2023, our wedding was fast approaching. It was planned for after I had finished the first year of my degree in August 2024. So far, the course has been amazing, emotional and stressful. There have been times when I wanted to give up and times when the 'mum guilt' was beating down on me.

Placement itself has been a rollercoaster. Being a student, especially a first-year student, can be difficult. Everyone's experiences have been different, but for me, the good has outweighed the bad. You can often lose sight of why you started doing something in the first place, and my first year would get like that sometimes for me. I had to ground myself and speak up when I felt that things were becoming too much at times, whether that was talking to Jake, my family, my uni friends or lecturers to offload. However, it's hard to explain unless someone has had experience with a healthcare degree and knows how much pressure is coming at you from all angles, not just in uni life but in *all* aspects. It's one big juggling act. But one I'll forever be grateful for.

In March 2024, I had the most incredible experience thrust upon me.

It was the Easter holidays. I had arranged extra shifts in advance for placement to make up some hours as my close friend's hen-do in Benidorm was arranged before I knew that I was successful at getting my place with uni. That was planned for May 2024 for three nights and four days; the dates clashed with placement.

It must have been fate. In a midwifery course, you must witness five births before you can start counting the births you have personally delivered. By then, I had already got my five witnesses to get 'hands-on,' as they say.

I was allocated a room where I would be working with a registered midwife. I walked in, and it was one of my *friends* in labour! I knew that she had been in for induction as she was updating us girls in our group chat on how things were progressing. But we hadn't heard from her in the past day; I assumed that I wouldn't be seeing her that day as she must still be waiting to come up to the labour ward. She knew that I was working, so she kept it as a surprise, but it was a total coincidence that I was allocated to her room.

I got my first delivery that day, which was even more special because it was my friend. It filled me with so much happiness that I could be with her in labour and that I was actually able to assist her in delivering her child. She will always hold a special place in my heart, as will her little baby, who's not so little anymore. We now have a bond we will always share. *Forever.*

During Easter break, it was also my hen-do. And what a fantastic hen-do it was. My mum, Jake's mum, our sisters and all my friends travelled on a party bus to York for the weekend. It was one of the best weekends of my life, filled with fun, laughter and a very embarrassing moment.

I won't go into too much detail about why it was embarrassing, but let's put it this way: I was caught out in a game of *Mr and Mrs* where my answers would have to match Jake's that he had completed before the hen-do and, if they didn't, I would end up dropping myself in it. And, to add to that, Jake's answers would also drop *me* in it, so I would basically be dropped in it *twice*; there was no real way for me to win! *How rude when it's YOUR weekend.*

We played more games, made cocktails, soaked in the hot tubs at our lovely accommodation, went out to bottomless brunch and hit York's town with a bang!

My bridesmaids and the mums had done me proud.

Seven weeks later, we were approaching the final three weeks of our placement block for uni, but Benidorm week had arrived. It was a very much welcomed break as it had been so full-on. It was amazing! My friend's bridesmaids had done her justice. We had a villa ten minutes away from the Benidorm strip in a taxi. It was absolutely gorgeous! We had a brilliant time full of laughs and drunken antics. *What happens in Benidorm stays in ben-i-d.....*

Okay, nothing *juicy* happened; only a minor inconvenience happened to me that was brought up in a speech by my bridesmaids on my wedding day. *Nobheads.* But I will not embarrass myself even more and divulge what MAY or MAY NOT have happened; *the end.*

Coming back from Benidorm, it was hard to get back into placement. I was so tired from the craziness of my friend's hen-do that it took me about a week to recover.

After a good few days, I got back into the swing of things. I completed my final few weeks of placement for year one, working on the labour ward. I managed to end the year by assisting twelve women in birthing their babies. What a magical feeling to see a baby being born. It's not always joyful, and some extremely sad cases had occurred. These are things out of anyone's control. Mother Nature can be so cruel. Even though I didn't directly witness a tragic outcome, it was hard not to be affected by one when it happened on the ward.

I have worked with absolutely fantastic midwives and learned so much from the various mentors that I have worked with. They excite students to become midwives themselves and encourage them to do more.

Placement finished in early June 2024. We only had four or five weeks left at university for the year, and I was looking forward to finishing. I was on the final wedding countdown but began to panic, thinking, perhaps wrongly, that I needed to sort my body out before the dress. I had been so busy with uni, my friend's hen-do and my own that I hadn't even thought about how I would look in my dress. It wasn't that I was huge, but I definitely wanted to trim up. Being on placement always sent me looking for quick sugar, and I think I had probably put a stone and 3 lbs on since summer 2023 (a year ago). Everyone has their own insecurities, and my weight is one of mine.

Time was ticking away— *time again, not being generous.*

I continued going to the gym throughout my first year at university. Still, it wasn't anywhere near what I had been before starting my degree, and my nutrition was way off. A quick fix was needed. Now that placement was out of the way, and I had completed all my assignments for the year, I could focus on a last-minute 'shredding for the wedding' phase. I lost half a stone and toned up a little before the big day.

One of the personal trainers at the gym, who had been helping me constantly since I had started going there in early 2023, knew of my student status and also of my upcoming wedding. We agreed to a 'smart' financial plan of 'worrying about payment at a later date', and he set about getting me in better shape for my big day. I worked hard in those last two months before my wedding, even though my friend's wedding was three weeks before mine and my second hen-do was in my hometown a week before.

That hen-do was incredible. We all wore 'shit shirts' that were all bright and colourful. Everyone also wore a bucket hat in honour of me (because I love them); I wore a veil the girls had got me for my York hen do. What a great day out that was!

At one point, I was standing on a bench in a bar with all of my hens and other random people singing with me while "*It's All Coming Back to Me*" by Celine Dion was playing. *Incredible vibes!* That quickly became a song that everyone at the hen associated with me and the wedding.

August 10th 2024, the day that I married my best friend. *He turned up!*

I couldn't believe that the day had arrived. I was so nervous, not about marrying Jake, but about having ninety-four sets of eyes on me while I walked down the aisle. Thankfully, I had my dad to hold on to.

My incredible dad made that day happen. He gave us a considerable amount of money for our special day, and my mum, stepdad and Jake's parents also contributed a hefty amount. It was money well spent if you ask me.

It was the best day of my life, besides the day that I birthed my son.

Everything was perfect and I didn't think twice about how I wasn't exactly where I wanted to be with my weight. I felt and looked like a princess.

There were many emotional moments shared that day. We toasted all the family and family friends who would have been there with us on our special day. We had a memory ladder with photographs of the loved ones to remember them.

My wedding colours were forest green, ivory and lilac. The lilac was in memory of Little Nana because it was her favourite colour. She would have adored the flowers! My wedding bouquet sits on my kitchen windowsill, and every time I look at it, I think of her. The flowers are silk so that I can have them forever.

Auntie Yvette and two of my cousins made it to my big day. My other cousin, who lives in America, couldn't make it as it would have been an expensive trip for him. They had a great time, considering that a huge personality was missing and who really should have been there: my uncle.

Frankie looked so handsome in his little suit, like his dad's. I was so proud of him and how he had done us proud by being our page boy.

I laughed, I cried, and my mates chanted "Jazzo" at various points throughout the day, which was just the icing on the cake. I danced the night away with my husband, family and friends. *"It's all coming back to me now"* was played, and it was epic!

I couldn't have asked for anything better.

So much credit is owed to Jake, my husband! It still feels strange to say that he is my husband, but it has only been a month since we got married at the time that I'm writing this. He has supported and cared for me in more ways than I can imagine. It must have been hard on him for the first few years of Frankie's life when I wasn't in the best mental shape; even when I thought that I was pushing him away, he just carried on loving me, *my caring, supportive husband.* He's also cared for my family, been a rock and comforted them through some of the hardest times that we have ever faced. Nothing is ever too much trouble for him; he has the purest soul that you could ever come across.

I am the luckiest girl in the world to have him by my side.

He's my happily ever after.

Always and forever.

I sit here finishing writing this book as a married woman, ready to start the next chapter of my life.

I have two more years of university ahead of me.

I know that I will face hurdles along the way, but I have the best team supporting me through every step of life and what it has to throw at me. I am lucky to have the people around me that I do.

I am fortunate.

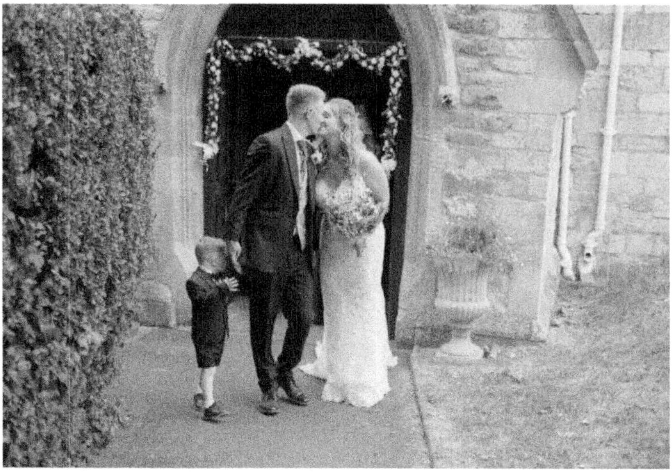

Dear Uncle Kev,

This is the first time that I've ever written a letter to someone, and I know that I won't get a reply. It's an odd thing to do, I suppose. Still, I have recently learnt that writing helps me articulate my feelings, so if it's okay, I will try it with my emotions about you.

What a man you were— a true legend in your own right and a real-life angel. You helped so many young kids who crossed your path when tutoring at college find a better way of life than the ones they were living. You have touched so many lives with your infectious personality, which everyone who knew you loved.

Firstly, I have to get this out of the way. I need to get my anger off my chest. It's been hard since you left. It is hard to watch my auntie, cousins, and mum endure the emotional and mental struggle. The pain that Nan and Grandad felt when they were alive was sickening. But I know that you three are together now, living in paradise, watching over us all and surrounding us with love.

You owe your sister a massive apology and a pat on the back for how she had to handle everything with Nan and Grandad when you left. Having to tell them the news that you had taken your own life was so cruel; I don't know how she managed it. Plus, there was everything that happened after with Grandad's dementia and having to put him in residential care because it was no longer safe for him to be at home. She needed you.

Then, my poor nana. Her world just kept getting turned upside down. It was such an awful time.

However, the most extensive apology needs to be saved for your wife. You have much grovelling to do when you see her again because she has been through hell. Plus, finding you the way that she did must have torn her apart from the inside. I am angry when I see her because her eyes show constant sadness, even when behind a smile. She will never be the same again; none of your family will, and I'm so mad at you for it.

Anyway, enough with the anger.

When Grandad passed, my friends bought a frame that said, "Because someone we love is in heaven, it means there is a bit of heaven in our home." I love it. It has a picture of you and Grandad together and takes pride of place on the best shelf in the house; as it should for two great men.

Nana has her place on my wall, and it's my favourite picture of her. She's smiling, holding Frankie when he was three months old, and it's so beautiful. That picture was taken on her first birthday without you. It must have been hard for her.

Auntie Yvette joined us and was battling so many emotions that day, but she still managed to play with Frankie and make him giggle. It made her smile, even if it was just for a few seconds.

Frankie is named after you and Grandad. His full name is Frankie John Fields, *John*, like your middle name and Grandad's first name. As you can tell, I managed to keep the tradition going of every family member having a name that begins with the letter 'J', just like you wanted.

But that would have been his name regardless.

He's an amazing little boy. He is a performer and loves an audience, just like his great-grandad, great-uncle... and his mother! He would have adored you and vice versa.

I like to believe that you drop by now and again to see us, all three of you. I bet you were so happy to see your mum and dad again; I can imagine the reunion was something special. I also like to think that you all would have been proud of what I have achieved. It's not been the most effortless ride, and there will be more obstacles to face. But I'm not giving up.

I hope that you, Nana, and Grandad enjoyed my wedding from your front-row seats. I especially hope that Nana liked the flowers! Your family was definitely missing you; well, all three of you... we *all* were. But they still managed to have a fantastic day, which was great to see.

Anyway, I won't go on. Just know that you are forever loved and gut-wrenchingly missed by many.

Until we meet again, unc; sleep tight.

Love, Jazz x

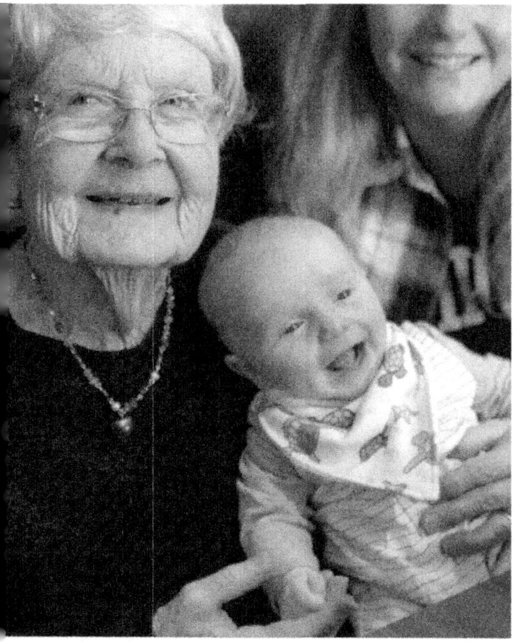

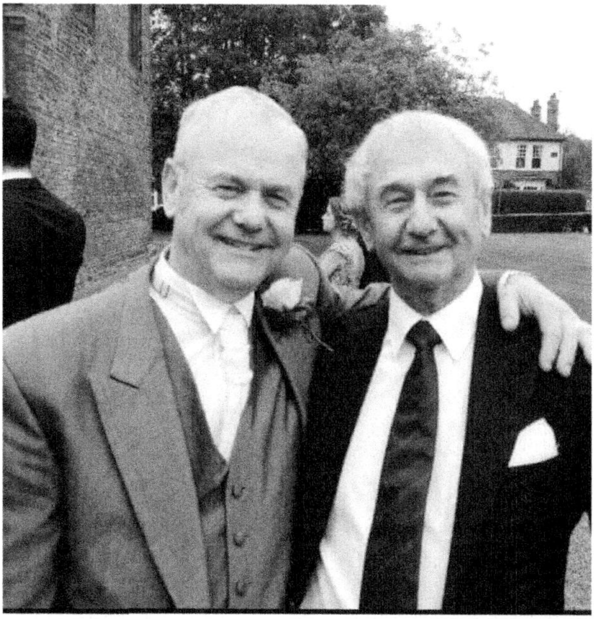

If any of the topics addressed in this book have affected you or someone you know and need help, here are some charities that offer support.

PTSD UK - a charity that supports people with post-traumatic stress disorder.

The Miscarriage Association - offers support to anyone affected by the loss of a baby in pregnancy.

PANDAS - A postnatal depression charity offering one-to-one support to women and their families affected by perinatal mental health.

Andy's Man Club - a male suicide prevention charity.

#ANDYSMANCLUB

SUICIDE IS THE BIGGEST KILLER OF MEN UNDER 45
1 MAN EVERY 2 HOURS

ALL OUR GROUPS MEET MONDAY 7PM

TO FIND YOUR NEAREST GROUP VISIT OUR WEBSITE
WWW.ANDYSMANCLUB.CO.UK

JOIN THE CONVERSATION
- info@andysmanclub.co.uk
- andysmanclub
- andysmanclubuk
- @andysmanclubuk

#ITSOKAYTOTALK

We are a peer to peer support group for men.
Come have a brew and a chat!

References

Florence + The Machine (2011). *Florence + The Machine - Shake It out*. Nashville., London., Santa Monica: EMI Blackwood Music Inc., Florence and the Machine Ltd., Universal Music Publishing Ltd.

Marley, B. (1980). *Bob Marley - Redemption Song*. [CD] Santa Monica: Universal Music Publishing.

Roiphe, A. (2008). *'Epilogue': Anne Roiphe On Becoming A Widow*. [online] NPR. Available at: https://www.npr.org/2008/12/23/98653632/epilogue-anne-roiphe-on-becoming-a-widow [Accessed 10 Sep. 2024].

Printed in Great Britain
by Amazon